LOVE *The*

FORMULA

How to Love...And Be Happier

CHARISSA JONES

Contents

The Love Formula vii

Introduction to The Love Formula ix

Gentle and Quiet 1

Forgiveness 18

Humble 28

Counsel 40

Patience 48

Trust 60

Truth 74

Discipline 85

Understanding 100

Love 112

References 131

Acknowledgments 133

About the Author 135

THE LOVE FORMULA

*L*ove is **gentle and quiet**; it speaks words of love and kindness and silences "fighting words."

Love is **forgiving**; it heals broken hearts and wounds; it is not afraid to say, "I'm sorry."

Love is **humble**; it believes we are equal and on this journey together.

Love **counsels**; it shares wise advice and listens.

Love is **patient**; it waits without complaint.

Love is **trusting**; it keeps its word and follows through.

Love is **truthful**; it shares its true feelings, dreams, hopes, and desires. It is authentic.

Love is **disciplined**; it stays on the path of love, relationship, and health.

Love **understands**; it continually asks questions to know one another through all of life.

Introduction to The Love Formula

The Qualities of Love

What does it mean to love and how do you show it?

What if learning how to love could save your most important relationships?

What if you could be happier and love every aspect of your life?

Has your heart ever been broken and you would like to forgive and move on?

Is trust an issue in your relationships?

Are there qualities about yourself that you wish you could change but don't know how?

What would it be like to practice love in all of your relationships and the relationship with yourself?

The Love Formula is a compilation of qualities that encompass and define what real love is and how to incorporate this true and genuine love into your life. Daily practice of each quality from the small to large occurrences in your life is the key. Each unique quality is best-practiced one-by-one to understand its real essence. Love is the root that fuels all of these qualities. From here on out, I will call these "pure qualities" because they are wholesome and timeless. They represent the beauty of all that is beautiful: nature, human love, and spiritual connection. When you practice these qualities in your life, you are practicing the very core qualities of what love is. Love embodies these qualities.

Before diving into each pure quality in detail, here is a brief overview. The first pure qualities are a duo, being gentle and quiet, a brilliant combination that will bring more love into your relationships. When you are gentle and quiet, with love, you are practicing love. Instead of yelling at someone for being mean to you, you express yourself in a gentle way. Additionally, you are slow to speak angry words by taking the time to think about how you feel. By being gentler and quieter, you will notice more around you and have fewer arguments. Wouldn't that be nice?

Next, having forgiveness is necessary for yourself, so you don't hold onto any anger that doesn't serve you. As issues occur in your life that call for forgiveness, know that everything is happening for a reason and that it's all rooted in love. You may not understand it now, but trust that forgiveness and acceptance are what you need. Loving forgiveness will open your heart to new possibilities.

As you practice being gentle, quiet, and forgiving, you will be humbled. To be humble is to be open to all that is available for you to learn. Being teachable will guide you on the path that you have always wanted to be on. Instead of closing yourself off with your pride, being humble will do the opposite. By listening to your inner knowing and the universal signs around you, you can trust that life is guiding you. The act of being humble will fill your spirit with love and joy because it is a pure quality that you were born to inhibit.

After folding these pure qualities into your daily life, others will begin to take notice. They will ask you questions about their life because they have seen a positive shift in yours. This is where your wise counsel comes into play. Counseling another needs a gentle and quiet nature because it requires active listening. When your friend has a tough decision ahead, and she comes to you to discuss and weigh her options, exercise these pure qualities to guide her through. As you genuinely listen, remember to give counsel with love.

Another very important pure quality is patience. There are many gifts of patience. While you're waiting in line at the store, you can notice all that is good around you: a man opening a door for a woman, a child smiling up at her daddy, the sun shining outside. Patience is a pure quality because it has so much to teach us. It guides us to being present. How many beautiful things have you missed because you weren't present? At times, it can feel like life is passing us by so quickly. Enjoying every moment and being present is the remedy for living life fully. Patience gives us this gift.

The following quality is trust; this is very personal and for many difficult. However, if there is love, then you can trust. This pure quality is so unique because life is about having relationships. As we know, relationships require trust for almost everything. For example, if you don't trust the person that you are in a relationship with it will cause problems. Your trust is required to function in this life from the small to serious conditions. As you discover each quality, you will find that each quality intertwines with each other as they are all the expressions of the powerful essence of love. For instance, when trust is broken, it requires forgiveness, and forgiveness requires wise counsel. Further, the act of being gentle and quiet will guide you to a peaceful place within.

Another precious quality is truthfulness. Being truthful with yourself and others is essential. It embodies the eternal wisdom of accepting reality for what it is. Acceptance and acknowledgment of reality are a gift. Further, being truthful with yourself and your loved ones builds trust. As human beings, we have the ability to lie, which leads to distrust and broken relationships. Sharing the truth with each other forms an everlasting bond.

All of these pure qualities have one thing in common, and that is that they are the core qualities of what love is. It's not to say that these qualities are easy to practice. It will be hard to be gentle and quiet when someone is yelling at you. It can be hard to forgive your husband if he comes home late after work three days in a row because he's busy playing golf with his friends. However, by practicing these qualities, it will become easier for you as they become a part of who you are. Ultimately, directing your relationships on the path of love.

While reading this book, begin practicing each quality with the smaller things. By practicing this way, a natural progression occurs of learning these qualities quickly. Be gentle and quiet for 20 minutes when you come home from work. Notice the different reactions you get from your family. Just by practicing these qualities on the smaller scale, they will build up inside of you and become a solid foundation for you. In this way, when something larger occurs in your life, you can easily handle it. After practicing being quiet when you return home, you may be more prepared when your best friend gets mad at you for not answering her phone calls. You will be calm, gentle, and quiet before explaining your legitimate reason. By having this quality more inside of you, you will be able to avoid a fight with your friend. Instead of instantly becoming defensive, you will take the time to be quiet, step back, and think about what you would like to say. It's the daily practice that is the most important because it is the easiest and will solidify the pure qualities within you.

All of these qualities need discipline. Many areas of your life require discipline. It takes discipline to wake up in the morning for work, visit the gym, cook healthy meals for your family, and keep a close connection to your spiritual life. Discipline is a pure quality because it is required for almost everything you do. With love, discipline is a beautiful quality because it brings structure and order to your life. Nature is our best example of structure and order, and it runs perfectly.

Lastly, love is understanding, and understanding is loving. How many times have you been upset by someone until you understood what was happening? Imagine that a woman is upset with her husband because he didn't call as she expected him to. When he comes home, she asks why he didn't call her. He tells her that he did call. He then proves it on his phone (however, the call never registered on her phone). When he called and she didn't answer, he figured she was busy. At least, she would see that he called and could call him back if she wanted. With a little bit of understanding, the situation was cleared.

Understanding should be your first line of defense. Almost every situation that needs mediation is because there is a misunderstanding. Many people have a hard time explaining their perspective. That's okay; be patient and take the time to understand their point of view. We all have different perspectives, and coming to an understanding will clear this up. Understanding takes love and patience.

Love is the beautiful life force of this world. It can create magnificent relationships. Practicing these pure qualities will teach you how to be more loving. They will guide you on a new path of freedom with ease and joy. This journey requires more love in every aspect of your life. Your relationships will change, and you will grow. You will expand into the loving person that you know you are. Love requires all of these pure qualities: gentle and quiet, forgiveness, humility, counseling, patience, trust, truthfulness, discipline, and understanding.

The discovery of these eternal and timeless qualities originated from my father, Dr. Ronald Alan Duskis. Not only was he a charming and intelligent man, but he also radiated love that everyone could feel instantly. He was the best example in my life of someone who was accepting of everyone. He treated every person the same. In his chiropractic practice, he would give his services for free to those who could not afford them because he genuinely wanted to help. Only with love is this type of altruistic behavior possible. He saw the importance of everyone and showed that everyone deserved as much love as possible.

He devoted his life to discovering the purpose of the Universe and the spiritual connection that we are all meant to have. His intuition and connection with the Universe gave him the ability to realize these qualities and practice them in his daily life. He was also a minister of a non-denominational church where his message was about these qualities and the importance of them to experience real love, with yourself and others. He saw how everything could and should be rooted in love. He saw that God in the Bible was a loving God, and His spirit was the essence of each of these qualities 100%.

The Love Formula isn't a religious book. Although my father isn't here in his physical body to continue sharing his message anymore, the qualities still hold an essential message. Incorporating the pure qualities with modern ideology sheds a new light and teaching.

The key to inner peace and a life full of joy is building these qualities into your character. You already have these qualities to a certain degree, and the potential for more is within you. Imagine feeling peace in every situation. Having the building blocks and a firm foundation in love, you will see expansion in every aspect of your life. The discovery of these qualities will bring about enlightenment that you are here to feel, know, and be, now. Let these qualities penetrate your everyday life. Hear the wisdom of their words which will bring the love and peace you are seeking. Besides your relationship with others, the pure qualities will teach you self-love, which is one of the reasons we are here on this earth. Learning to love yourself is part of your purpose. Lastly, have as much fun as possible practicing these qualities.

Gentle and Quiet

*Love is gentle and quiet; it speaks
words of love and kindness and
silences fighting words.*

*T*he pure qualities, gentle and quiet, are life changing. The act of being gentle and quiet is to practice thinking and speaking with kindness toward yourself and others. It is the act of being in a calm state. Have you ever noticed how many times you have said something regretfully? What about the harsh words you can still recall your loved one saying to you? If only you were able to take the time to think before you spoke; how many fights would be minimized and relationships intact?

The pure qualities are the actual makeup of love. The essence of each quality is a distinct piece of the puzzle to bring peace and love to Earth. One of these pieces is being gentle and another is being quiet. As you practice being gentle and quiet, positive relationships will build with everyone around you, including yourself. As you can imagine, this process is, transformative. Not only will you hear more, but you will also experience more of life around you.

Right now, what do you see around you that looks gentle and quiet? Your dog or cat may be resting on the couch peacefully. Notice, the surrounding calmness and quietness. The act of being gentle and quiet lets you notice everything around you, and when you are doing that, you are present. When the force of presence takes hold, all of life is more beautiful. This gentle and quiet nature is the peace that will manifest deep within your spirit and knowing. It will feel calm, loving, and spacious. As the world spins quickly around you, you have the ability to pause, feel, smile, and love. All of this is yours to experience by being gentle and quiet.

The best time to practice being gentle and quiet is when you are angered or annoyed. These are the times when it is easiest to snap, either with words or with a disapproving face. Instead, utilizing the gentle and quiet nature can be a tool to refrain from saying or doing anything that you may regret.

Have you ever felt guilty after yelling at someone? Feeling guilty after an interaction is your guilt-sensor. It is letting you know that what you have done or said isn't in line with love. We all have a guilt-sensor. This is where, in retrospection, you feel sorry or guilty for speaking a certain way or doing something unkind. This sensor may not kick in right away, but it will always tell you if you have done something against your moral beliefs. In hindsight, you see that being gentle and quiet would have been a better option.

Being in an intimate relationship will bring up many areas to practice this quality. I am married to a hard-working and passionate man, Nate. Our relationship continues to grow positively as we grow. The love we have for each other is special, and I couldn't have asked for a better partner. Every day our relationship grows as different situations arise. There are many aspects of relationship and with that, they are constantly morphing and changing. Incorporating the pure qualities helps us to grow our relationship with the foundation of love. In any relationship, there is continual learning of what love is and how it can be expressed between the two of you.

When Nate and myself were picking out a color to paint our bedroom, he let me know he would be happy with any shade but maroon. A week later I asked him again what that color was because I couldn't remember. He became frustrated with me because I was asking a question I had already asked, and he answered. His annoyance wasn't that I was asking the question but that he felt I wasn't listening to him the first time around. When he expressed his frustration, I remained gentle and quiet. A few minutes later, he said he was sorry but aggravated because we had already discussed the paint color a few days earlier. To him, it looked like I hadn't been paying attention. Additionally, he expressed that when I didn't listen, it gave him the message that I didn't care because I was not present with him. This example is two-fold: his guilt-sensor kicked in without my needing to say anything, and it was a reminder for me to be more present.

If your significant other gets irritated with you (and it will happen), know that you don't have to react to it; practice being gentle and quiet instead. This way you honor yourself, and you deliver love to the situation. Further, a fight will be mitigated. The primary aspect of this is that you don't need to bring attention to the situation. Their guilt-sensor will let them know if they weren't nice. Trust in this and give yourself space to love through the gentle and quiet nature.

Here is a secret to a happy life: *Allow the inner knowing of the other person to manifest without having to be the disciplinary or teacher.* Being the disciplinary only makes you look and feel bad. Besides, the other person will most definitely shut their ears to what you are saying. This inner voice is within all of us, which will let the other person know if what they said wasn't kind. It will guide the other person to this realization. Similarly, your inner voice will nudge you if you have said something that wasn't kind. The inner voice is a compass, and everyone has one. You can learn to trust it as it takes a load off of your shoulders because you no longer need to put effort into telling others how they have hurt you. Their inner voice will let them know. All you need to do is just be your loving, kind, and gentle self.

Usually, you can detect in people's voices if they are upset, happy, nervous, etc. When angry, it is hard to mask it with a pleasant tone. Feeling this way makes it tough to speak peaceful words. Therefore, it is best to practice the gentle and quiet qualities and refrain from speaking right away. The Love Formula emphasizes that love silences fighting words. This is when the pure quality of quietness plays a significant role. Try this out, and if it's too hard, then try it on something smaller. Think about if it is worth saying what you want to say. Words are powerful and can be very harmful if loaded with angry emotions. Of course, there are times to speak, but with awareness of what you really want to say and how you are feeling without loaded statements that may cause a fight. A pure quality mantra is this: *You will feel more at peace when you give yourself time to think about how you feel and what you would really like to say.*

As you are about to embark on this journey, you may find your former self at odds with the newer self you are becoming. For years, you have been one way, and now you are transforming yourself, for the better, in another way. This will take convincing of your former self to become renewed. For example, your old self may try to convince you that saying what is on your mind is standing up for yourself. She may disagree with being gentle and quiet. However, your newer self may see the benefit. She may decide that by not expressing yourself, this time, you will avoid an unnecessary fight.

Most of the time, fighting words do not get you anywhere. They are just a detriment to the relationship and have no added benefit. However, speaking your mind in a gentle, calm tone does have benefits. It brings peace of mind, healthy relationships, and more love in all aspects of your life. The occasional setbacks are necessary to reinforce why you are creating this change in your life. Each setback is a reminder of why you only want to move forward and how destructive your past actions were. Life is a process. The Love Formula is a life process. Through it, you will gain the tools necessary to have a life full of love and trust.

These qualities will become a part of who you are, and they will be unique to your personality and character. Developing each quality inside of you according to *your* life is what's important. When you begin to practice being gentle and quiet, it will be your way. You may find yourself censoring what you say in a group setting or finding time in your day for meditation. The quietness you find should only be to your benefit and not used for harm. You should not silence yourself when you need to speak; instead, think about what you really would like to say before saying it.

Each one of us wants and needs to be heard. Sometimes that can be difficult when everyone, including you, is consumed in his or her bubble. I remember a fight I had with my loved one. The next day I didn't remember much of what he had said. Being consumed in my world of problems I didn't stop to think about his. How could I be closer to a loved one without stepping out of my bubble and trying to understand his? I needed to hear and understand his perspective. Practicing the quality of quietness, in this situation, would have been a benefit as it would've led me on the right path to listening and considering his perspective.

Among the most influential powers in your life are the most silent: your thoughts. Your thoughts shape and mold your words and actions. Without even realizing it, your thoughts shape who you are and what you will do next. As you begin to become aware of your thoughts, you will experience how influential they are. Your thoughts lead to your actions. As a test of this, try to think of something opposite. The classic example is when someone asks you not to visualize a pink elephant. What do you end up seeing? A pink elephant! To go a little deeper, think a loving thought toward your best friend. Do you feel like doing something nice for them? As soon as you change your thoughts, you also change your actions, and in return, your new thoughts will now pave the way for a different action. Ultimately, you have control over your thoughts. You have the ability and power to create your future.

Consider focusing your thoughts on how you would like your future to be. Does it contain more love in your relationships? Adventure? Peace and quiet? Your thoughts need to match up to obtain more of that in your life. To have more love, think loving thoughts. To have more adventure, think adventurous thoughts; by thinking this way, you will be more aware of adventurous opportunities.

Have you ever realized that when you are on vacation, you are a different person? Are you more relaxed, happy, and open to new experiences? What kind of thoughts are you thinking about when you are on vacation? My friend, Samantha, was telling me that she always looks her best on vacation. She knows that it's because she is filling her days and thoughts of all the adventure she is having. She loves to scuba dive, drink margaritas, enjoy good food, and relax on the beach. She has focused her attention and thoughts on the things that make her happy, and in turn, she glows and looks her best.

How can every day be like this for you? Consider taking "vacation thought breaks" throughout your day. Imagine relaxing on a beach, taking a walk in nature, or laying down on a soft bed for a few minutes. Instantly, your body will relax, and you will probably find a smile on your face. What a gift it is to choose your thoughts at any moment.

You have an internal dialogue that no one can hear but you. You can express these inner thoughts to the outside world if you choose. There is a gift in being able to express your views outwardly, but it can also be a detriment. A pure quality mantra is this: *Words can uplift or bring down. Think before you speak.*

Thoughts can either bring you up or down. Mental and physical quietness play an essential role in everyone's life, and it is important to acknowledge. Having the time to be quiet is revitalizing as it gives your mind rest. It is the same when you wake up in the morning from a restful sleep. This "time off" is needed for your body and mind. After this rest, your brain and body are reset.

If you are a morning person, most likely you feel energized and renewed when you wake up. You may especially notice a difference if you had an exhausting day previously. Taking a break, mentally and physically, during the day is also important. Just as it is essential to rest every evening, it will have the same benefit if you take a break during the day. Try squeezing in a few minutes for deep breathing, positive affirmations, or just closing your eyes and silencing your thoughts. Some of my greatest ideas have come just after doing one of these activities.

Thoughts influence actions and feelings. Thinking the thought that you are tired will make you feel more tired than you are. Conversely, thinking invigorating thoughts will energize you. For example, when exercising, say, "I have energy! I am strong!" and see a difference in your energy and strength. Your thoughts have great influence. Most likely, your energy and posture will perk up and motivate you to finish strong.

Most of our thoughts stem from beliefs that we have learned over time. Listen to your thoughts and then question them. Why did you just say what you said out loud? What were your thoughts before you spoke? Attempt to listen to your thoughts before you communicate. Check if what you're about to say comes from a place of love or fear. You can be confident in what you have to say if it comes from a place of love.

As your thoughts occur, they can make you happy or sad. Thankfully, you have the choice to listen, change, and choose your thoughts. Your thoughts are your silent motivator. And so, words are your way of motivating others. Your words can have a significant impact on others. People listen to people. Speaking words of encouragement will help others be and do better. Everyone can use a friend to encourage them. By using your words, you can influence and make positive changes in other people's lives.

My sister, Christina Duskis, has written a book called *Your Body Relationship*. While she was writing it, there were tough times to complete it, as you can imagine. As a family member, I encouraged her to keep going. I let her know that her message was unique and wanted. I let her know that I, and so many others, needed to hear it. She finished that book, and when it was published, it became a best-seller on Amazon. I highly recommend it! More information about her methodology and book can be found at www.ChristinaDuskis.com.

Her love and passion for this topic would have kept her going without my encouragement, but my words gave her a push to persevere. This type of support, whether it is from a friend or spouse, is so important in life. This connection with others is the life force of productivity;

encouragement leads to development. Next time a friend is struggling or questioning his life, reassure him. Let him know that you believe in him and his abilities.

Your words are powerful. However, your actions speak more than a thousand words. There is a powerful movie called *Girl Rising*. It is about girls struggling in poverty-stricken lands. In this film, a girl takes off her veil that covers her face and climbs to the top of a hill; this was forbidden for her. All the other girls in the field follow her lead and do the same thing (Robbins, 2013).

She doesn't speak one word; there isn't a compelling, motivational speech. It was her action that moved the other girls to follow her lead. With that one act, she changed her life and empowered the lives of those girls around her. Action, with the absence of words, can have a significant influence on others. This girl was an example that quietness is meaningful work. Her opinion about her situation was heard without words.

When quieting your mind, you give yourself space for communication to occur between yourself and the Universe. You will be able to hear new realizations that may not have been heard with your current thoughts in the forefront. When it is most quiet for you, take the time to connect with the Universe. It always has a special message for you. It may gently nudge you to call a friend, plan a much-needed vacation, or pursue a life-changing job opportunity.

Many times we react to a situation with words without thinking before speaking. All of our words come from a belief system that we have. These beliefs may or may not be true for you. In other words, you probably have a lot of beliefs that you have learned from others, especially your parents. Your thinking patterns (or principles) have been ingrained in you. By questioning your thoughts, a shift will occur in your belief system. Hearing your authentic self will give you the ability to align with who you are at your core. Feelings are similar and with quietness in your heart, you can discover how you truly feel.

Meditation is an excellent catalyst for creating inner calmness. Sitting quietly and listening to your breath gives the mind time to clear itself of its thoughts. By doing this, gentleness increases within you. Further, one of the benefits is calming your mind of worry and anxiety that you may have. Worrying is a form of energy. This energy takes away from gentleness and inner peace.

Try listening to your breath and calming your thoughts whenever you can. As you listen to your breath, repeat a pure quality on the inhale. For example, breathe in *joy, trust, forgiveness, truth*. As you do this, you are changing your energy to that of the pure quality. They are pure and carry the energy of love, which will feel so good to your spirit.

As you begin to practice being quiet, you will discover a whole new world. One day, as I took notice of the quietness that surrounded me, calmness existed on an entirely new level. I felt joy, peace, and love intertwined with the quietness. I went to a beautiful place to experience this serenity: the botanical gardens in the middle of Denver. At first, my mind had a lot of thoughts, but as I became aware of them and quieted them down, I began to notice other things such as the conversations of people around me, the different smells, and the small insects flying busily around me; my other senses came alive.

As I began my journey around the garden, the gentle and quiet nature of the plants and flowers surrounded me. They play a crucial role in the survival of man and animals. They exist as a calm and non-intrusive part of life. As they should, they flowed naturally in their surroundings. Stepping farther away from the plants I could see that they held a simplistic beauty, but up close the details of each plant and the busyness of the insects thrived. Although the insects were busy with their duties, they did it in a calm manner as if the way they were was the way they should always and will be. They continued their tasks, regardless of the people walking around them, as to not disturb their natural cycle. They did not let the busyness or disturbances around them stop what they were doing. They truly were gentle and quiet.

Looking in on this living world of insects and foliage, I thought about what the opposite would look like if the insects were not gentle and quiet. The world would be much more chaotic if nature didn't continue with its natural order. Thankfully, we can walk by a tree that is flowering, and the birds and bees continue with what they are doing without attacking. (Of course this isn't true all of the time, but most of the time.) The point is that their nature is gentle and quiet and not easily aroused to anger.

What would this look like for a man who is not gentle and quiet? He would be easily disturbed by anyone coming into his personal space. It would be hard for him to continue to feel peaceful with what he is doing when disturbed. He is quick to attack with words or an annoyed facial expression. His individual order does not exist when upset. He does not have complete gentleness inside his spirit.

In contrast, one who is gentle and quiet would be like the birds and bees, unruffled by outside disturbances. She is calm, knowing her purpose in life. This woman is without strife or disorder. She is gentle and quiet as nature is, continuing with her business of the day.

When building these qualities into your life, you will find a very natural way of being just as this gentle and quiet woman. The gentleness flowing through you will bring you peace in every situation. You were created to flow with life and not against it.

Nature, humans, and animals have a continuous flow among themselves. The energy is shared. As you emanate gentleness, you will receive gentleness. It is similar to getting a massage. As the masseuse gently massages and relaxes your muscles; they are transferring that touch and feeling to you physically and emotionally. There is a transfer of energy between the two of you.

Further, if you want to connect with the gentleness and quietness of nature, submerse yourself in it. Spend time with a cuddly dog or cat to connect with their gentle and quiet flow. The energy is always there if you would like to partake in it. It is the human that has the choice to flow with or without this energy. What choice will you make? As you can be with nature and animals to receive their gentle and quiet nature, being this yourself will also spread that energy to others around you. What a gift that you can be!

There is also a time to be firm, but this can be done in a gentle way. For example, when a child is about to run in the middle of a street, then is the time to be firm. While being firm, you can be gentle, so you don't harm a child emotionally.

Being gentle should not be confused with being weak, soft-spoken, or wimpy. Instead, every situation calls for gentleness even during hard times. For example, when you are in an argument, fewer hurtful words will be spoken when taking the gentle approach. The same principle applies to physical activity. For example, when lifting weights, you need to be gentle on your body as to not injure it. Further, when out with friends, you can be gentle with yourself spiritually by not talking poorly about yourself or others. Gentleness is a pure quality that is meant to bring life and is, therefore, everlasting. Only value comes from this quality.

As an intricate being, you are equipped with the answers to life's situations. You have the ability to access this wisdom and knowledge. Begin your journey into quietness by being still when you are not. Listen to your thoughts. Then, ask the questions that you are seeking the answers for. The answers will come when you allow them to. Amazingly, you will give the space for your creative nature to get through when you are still. Trust that the answers are coming, and wait. The answers always come, and the peace is always there waiting for you.

Let me give you an easy example. It is a Sunday afternoon, and you are looking for something to do. Ask yourself these questions: *What would be fun for me to do right now? What will feel light for my spirit? Who would be great to see?*

Then, relax and know that the answers are heading your way. It may come in the form of a soft voice in your head or a phone call from a friend with an invitation. When I asked these questions last Sunday, I had a great time. My friend, Sara, asked me if I would like to visit a winery nearby. Of course, I said yes! The winery was on a beautiful ranch with many horses. We tasted wine, ate fresh strawberries, and had fun girl talk. It was fantastic! After that, I had another new friend invite me to her place to watch a television show. We ended up chatting for a couple of hours, laughing, and having fun. Needless to say, the questions work, and I hope you try them out, soon.

We all want to be heard. Therefore, listen to others and give them the chance to speak what is on their mind. You never know what wisdom they have to teach you.

When my friend and I would get together to chat on the phone, usually I dominated the conversation. I was just so excited to tell him everything that was going on in my life. I would get off the phone and think, *What is going on in his life?*

After this realization, the next phone call, I listened to him. I learned about many interesting things going on in his life. He expressed things to me that I had never heard him express before. I was enlightened and forever changed. Listening to him was a benefit to our relationship. What person in your life do you talk more than you listen? Next time you talk to them, let them speak and actively listen to them.

As you begin to explore the quality of quietness, you will notice that many people talk, just to talk. With so many thoughts running through their head, many automatically say every one of them or at least whichever ones get their attention enough to be spoken. This isn't necessarily a bad thing, but something to notice in others and yourself. Is it a benefit to share every thought that you are having?

Does it help to hear every thought that someone else is having?

Today I had lunch with my old friend Lucy. She loves to talk. I would say that she has a gift. As I sat listening to her, I gained a deeper respect for being quiet. As the two hours proceeded, I listened as she spoke about anything and everything that came to her mind. I learned a lot about her, which was splendid, but she didn't learn anything about me. Neither did I have the chance to comment on what she was sharing or share about myself.

At the end of our get together, she said, "Oh my, I've talked the whole time and haven't heard how life is going for you, I'm so sorry. How is it going?"

As I proceeded to speak, she interrupted and continued with her thought process that I just reminded her about. It was a fantastic display of control by our thoughts and the power they can have over one's mind and words. Even though I was able to practice listening, this situation with Lucy happened every time we met. I learned to accept and prepare myself mentally. I knew that by being quiet, I was giving her the opportunity to be expressive. A simple pure quality mantra is: *When quiet, the opportunity for others to be expressive presents itself.*

There is passive and active listening. For example, when Lucy asked me a question and then reminded herself about a story she wanted to share, that was passive listening. She was preparing for what she would say next instead of hearing what I had to say and then responding to that. Actively listening to someone is one of the real joys of being quiet. This involves being entirely present and listening without interruption. It is waiting for the other person to finish without forming a response. It is a learned skill, and it comes with many gifts.

The gift of active listening is that you get to learn from others, and vice versa. We can't experience all circumstances in life. Therefore, you can share and learn from each other instead. Nobody has a dull life, but everybody has experiences with wisdom gained. It is a life-giving quality to fully listen as someone expresses himself or herself. Although I may not have had the opportunity to share my stories with Lucy, I did learn that quietness gives the opportunity for others to be expressive.

Gentleness and quietness are pure qualities that benefit every aspect of your life. There is a time to be quiet and a time to speak. There is a time to be gentle and a time to be firm. There is a harmonious balance that exists between these qualities. As these develop, you will have time to reflect on how you feel about things, what you want out of life, and, most of all, gain a sense of peace in all you do and encounter over time. You will attain wisdom from yourself and others as you listen. Overall, you will feel the peace of knowing that you can handle any situation with clarity and calmness of mind.

✦

FORGIVENESS

━━━◦❲❤❳◦━━━

*Love is forgiving; it heals broken
hearts and wounds; it is not
afraid to say, "I'm sorry."*

━━━◦❲❤❳◦━━━

I have found that forgiving others and myself is a huge part of my daily life. We all make mistakes or will do and say things that will hurt someone else. An apology can help mend those wounds between relationships. For example, a friend may be in a bad mood and treat you poorly. This is the time to forgive him because we have all been in a bad mood and have hurt another because of it. Another example is when someone cuts you off while driving. Who knows what's going on in the other person's head? Are they personally trying to upset you? Probably not. Did they do something that warrants an apology? Of course! However, you most likely are not going to get one, because they are driving in another car and you are not going to go and chase them down. Although you are angry with them for cutting you off, there isn't much you can do, except forgive and move on. You can hold onto this anger, or you can know that you have probably cut someone off before too, not knowing, because you were in a rush.

These types of situations are not unusual and most everyone has been cut off or yelled at and vice versa. However, when the tables are turned, it provokes anger. When this happens, remember that you have been on the other side. It is then that you needed to be forgiven. It is the act of forgiveness that is so freeing. It will give you the space to let go and be present in the moment and not the past. Staying stuck in the past only harms you because there isn't anything you can do about it. The past is out of your control. The only thing that exists is what is occurring at that moment. Letting go is one of the most powerful tools to having a happy life. It's also one of the hardest and easiest things to do. All it takes is one decision to let go.

When it comes to forgiveness, ask this one question, *Why not forgive?*

Personally, if I don't forgive right away, anger and resentment build up inside of me, which only hurts the relationship I am in and me. The anger will come out in other ways until I forgive the wrong I believed was done. Forgiveness is the key to a lasting, peaceful relationship with yourself, others, and the world around you.

To forgive, you must let go of the part of you that is trying to protect you. This part tells you that you have been wronged and you have every right to be angry. This part is warning you to keep your distance so you are not hurt again. You are trying to protect yourself. But by doing this, you are closing the lines of communication and building a stone wall between others and yourself.

In the television show *Revenge,* the main character, Emily, loses her father to a terrorist attack that was set up by another family. They all live in the Hamptons and have a lot of money. They use their wealth and connections to manipulate and get what they want. Emily is seeking revenge for her father's setup and murder. Therefore, she sets up the people who had a hand in her father's demise. She is full of hate. In the end, she finds the actual man who murdered her father. She's about to kill him when she has a memory of herself with her dad on the beach. He says, "I love how you always find the good in everyone. Promise me you will always find the good in everyone."

She answers, "I promise."

At that moment, she let's go of the man she is about to murder. She chooses to keep her promise to her father above her agenda for revenge. In this dramatic story of revenge, there is only hurt and betrayal. The main character is hurting others and herself by not forgiving (Revenge, 2011-2015).

Revenge is a painful, destructive path to go down. It hurts others, but most of all it hurts you. Holding onto anger is damaging to your thoughts and surrounding life. Forgiveness is essential to letting go and being free from undesirable feelings.

Forgiveness dissipates anger and puts things into perspective. Why be angry when you can be happy? As the famous London playwright, Oscar Wilde said, "Always forgive your enemies—nothing annoys them so much" (Wilde, 1854-1900).

On a more thoughtful note, William Ward, a notable author, states, "Forgiveness is a funny thing. It warms the heart and cools the sting" (Ward, 1921-1994).

Not only does forgiveness heal a hurting relationship but it also releases the personal pain of anger inside that is not good for anyone to hold onto. Releasing resentment mainly helps you and then, as a result, helps the relationship.

Forgiveness is a quality that requires a lot of strength. Not very many people can forgive easily. It takes a new perspective to understand the situation. People have their own perspective on how a situation has happened. Trying to understand the other person's perspective can be difficult. However, it does shed light on a situation. And, that will help to figure out why the person acted the way they did.

Remember a time when you have been forgiven. What about when you have forgiven someone else? After forgiveness happens your relationships will begin the journey to healing. The perceived wrong that was done to you and that you did to another does benefit from the act of forgiveness. Once you forgive, the pain and anger will dissipate. You can move on and look at the present and future instead of the past. Anger about a wrong in the past is exactly that—in the past. Most of the time it can be hard to let go and forgive because then you may feel that you are allowing it to happen again. It feels as though you are giving permission to the person to repeat what was done. This is not true. Instead, you are allowing healing to occur in the damaged relationship.

If the person is sorry, you can choose to accept their apology. The decision is always yours. If they make the same mistake again, you can choose to forgive them again. Remember that it is for your own personal healing and the healing of the relationship. Further, you always have the right to leave the situation.

Forgiveness is not always easy. There are times when a cooling down period needs to be taken after a big fight. Also, time, energy, and understanding need to be taken into consideration before forgiving. Usually, the longer it takes, the greater the forgiveness needed. If someone accidentally bumps into you while walking on the street and then apologizes, it is easy to forgive and forget. If a spouse cheats on you, it is much harder and most likely impossible to ever forget, but possibly with enough time, you can forgive. Even then, divorce happens due to the inability to forgive. Many live their daily lives with the burden of an infidelity on their shoulders. Possibly they would like to forgive and forget, but they find it too difficult. The measure of the pain runs deep. When forgiveness is possible, however, it will heal your heart and give you peace of mind. It is only one choice—your—choice, away from happening.

Once you have established that forgiving is vital to inner peace, you can begin the process. Remember, you don't need to forgive overnight. It may even take years, but the work will be healing and worth it. Here is a step-by-step process for forgiveness:

1. Say, "I forgive (name)."
2. Ask the Universe to help you forgive from your heart.
3. Try to understand the perspective of the person and the situation.
4. Repeat as many times as necessary.

Each time you practice this process, you will forgive a little more and the healing process will begin.

Some belief systems say that forgiveness is not needed because right and wrong don't exist. They say that there are no rules, only points of view. In this way, right and wrong don't exist, but only in the construct of our beliefs. I agree with this thinking to an extent; however, beliefs do exist for everyone. Belief systems run deep within the core of humanity and give shape to who people are. These views are truth and right and wrong exists from these. Therefore, when a "wrong" is done, it is important to understand the other person's point of view. The "wrong" that was done is a point of view and may not have been a deliberate "wrong."

For example, Jack and Lauren were arguing over what time to take Jack to the airport the next morning. Jack believed that they should get to the airport 2 ½ hours before the flight. He got defensive when Lauren said she felt that was too much time. Jack felt "wronged" that Lauren didn't trust his judgment and desire to be at the airport earlier. Lauren felt "wronged" that he didn't consider her calculation. She also felt like he didn't care about her sleep. After discussing where their beliefs stemmed from they were able to come to an understanding. They ended up compromising but the main point is that they were able to understand each other's points of view. Neither was "wronged" even though they both felt that way in the beginning.

Forgiveness is a powerful tool. It gives us the ability to be in the moment by forgetting about the past. It provides us with the guidance to be in peace and harmony with the Universe instead of discord with a previous incident. As we learn to forgive, even the little things, we will blossom into our true nature because we are in the present moment. As the famous philosopher, Omar Khayyam says, "Be happy for this moment. This moment is your life" (Khayyam, 1048-1131).

Consider how forgiveness would free you in your life and bring more love into your relationships. Additionally, as we explore the gift of forgiveness and how it is a pure quality, it needs to be rooted in love for its remarkable impact.

There are many ways to apologize; one of them is to say, "You're right, I'm wrong."

Sometimes you may not even see how you are "wrong" and maybe you aren't, but just saying this can help to remedy the situation. This way the other party can let their defenses down and talk through the problem with you, regardless if you think you are right or wrong. Remember, right and wrong exist within the constructs of your belief system. What is wrong to you may be right to someone else. The point is to get to a healthy space of communication.

Of course, the right way to apologize is important. In *When Sorry Isn't Enough*, coauthors Gary Chapman and Jennifer Thomas explain that "The key to good relationships is learning the apology language of the other person and being willing to speak it. When you speak their primary language, you make it easier for them to genuinely forgive you. When you fail to speak their language, it makes forgiveness more difficult because they are not sure if you are genuinely apologizing" (Chapman & Thomas, 2013).

Speaking the right apology language is, therefore, crucial if you want it to mean anything to the other person. Each person hears a particular type of apology the best and some they won't even hear at all. Further, they state, "When one's sense of right is violated, that person will experience anger. He or she will feel wronged and resentful at the person who has violated their trust. The wrongful act stands as a barrier between the two people, and the relationship is fractured. They cannot, even if they desired, live as though the wrong had not been committed" (Chapman & Thomas, 2013).

Some people will say that they don't care or they don't need an apology, but then why is there an unsettled feeling inside when there is an issue?

Apologizing is accepting responsibility for our behavior. Mending any offense when possible leads to a more peaceful and healthy relationship. If you are truly sorry and would like to make amends then why not? As coauthors, Gary Chapman and Jennifer Thomas say, "A sincere apology and genuine forgiveness open the door to the possibility of trust growing again" (Chapman & Thomas, 2013).

Trust is vital in any relationship. We are continually putting our confidence in others to get anything done. For example, I have to trust Nate that he's not going to steal or destroy my personal belongings in the house that we share. Without that trust, we couldn't be building the house and home we love so much. Further, I believe that Nate would protect me if I were ever in harm. If I didn't trust him, then our relationship would suffer drastically. I wouldn't know if I should lock all of my things up in a safe or sleep with one eye open. That would be ridiculous, a hassle, and definitely not any fun.

Gary Chapman and Jennifer Thomas list the five languages of apology in *When Sorry Isn't Enough*. I will give a brief summary; however, I highly encourage reading the book for more detail and stories. Also, I recommend visiting their website, http://www.5lovelanguages.com, where you will find a profile for discovering your own language of apology. You can find it at http://www.5lovelanguages.com/profile/apology/.

1. Expressing regret; I apologize.
2. Accepting responsibility; I was wrong.
3. Making restitution; What can I do to make it right?
4. Genuinely repenting; I'll try not to do that again.
5. Requesting forgiveness; Will you please forgive me?

Each apology language is specific to an individual and what they believe is a sincere apology. The healing process includes learning the other person's apology language. What is your apology language? Once you know what yours is, let your significant other know. This gives him the option, when he apologizes, for it to be fully accepted. If one is going to apologize, it might as well be in the language that the other person can hear and understand. You wouldn't speak Italian to your husband if he doesn't speak that language. This is the same type of concept; speak his apology language so he can understand you and forgiveness can take place.

Lastly, let's practice another way to come to forgiveness. I learned this method from Louise L. Hay's book, *You Can Heal Your Life*. In it she says to say the following, "I forgive

_____ for _____. I forgive myself for _____" (Hay, 1984).

For example, "I forgive my husband for snapping at me about my driving. I forgive myself for being hard on myself."

Just saying this relieves tension. Words are powerful. Just as a negative statement has weight so does a positive one. Saying a forgiveness statement such as the one suggested by Hay will have a positive outcome. Allow that to guide you into a positive feeling about the particular situation.

Who do you need to forgive to feel free? Is there a certain event that has happened in your life that may be holding you back? I suggest practicing the forgiveness statements. By just saying them out loud, your subconscious will know who and what to bring up at the time. Your spirit is a magnificent, all-knowing awareness that will guide you to love and forgiveness.

Humble

Love is humble; it believes we are
equal and on this journey together.

Being humble can be a tough process for mostly everyone. It requires allowance of being open to learning from others. Most of the time people want to impose their own ideas, beliefs and opinions on you. In this way, they can show how much they know and feel important. This is the opposite of being humble and instead is the ego being prideful. Many people will argue over trivial things just to be right. Once I was arguing over which direction was true north. The debate went on for about 10 minutes. It turns out I still don't know which one of us was right. The point is that we both wanted to be right, and we argued about it for too long.

"You're right, and I'm wrong," is a powerful statement.

I'm positive that if I had said to the person who was arguing with me over which direction was north, "You're right, and I'm wrong," the debate would have ended.

Why? Because the only point of the discussion was to be and feel correct, which couldn't have ended well. Instead, being humble is about being open to learning from others. If the other person were right, I would have learned something new: that North was in a different direction than I'd thought. How many things are you shutting yourself off to because of certain limiting beliefs that you have and are not open to learning from others?

Humbleness includes being open to instruction for the betterment of the relationship and yourself. Being prideful is the opposite of being humble. Having a prideful attitude can hurt the ones around you because you are elevating yourself above them. My co-worker Alex was full of pride in everything he did. He made sure to let everyone know how good he was. He never backed down from a fight and always stuck an argument out until the end. Needless to say, he didn't make friends quickly. People didn't feel good when they were around him; they felt judged and inferior to him. Alex wasn't very humble but prideful.

On the other hand, confidence and letting others know your abilities is a beautiful gift for you to share. We all have talents and gifts to contribute to this world. However, we don't need to be so full of pride that we are only focused on ourselves. Focus on what everyone has to offer, including you. See the gift in yourself and everyone else. And lastly, uplift yourself and others with love. This is the key to a humble life. You can be noticed, have incredible talent, and share them with the world. Allow your gifts to shine through with love and humbleness.

Having humility is when you can truly see who you are; it is the base of who and what you are at your core. This exists when you remove any beliefs or cultural norms of how you should be. The world has put an exhausting amount of requirements on everyone—one must be a certain way to be accepted and loved. Who you are without this cultural blanket is beautiful, precious, and innocent. Your core self, also known as your inner being, will not betray you; allow it to lift you.

At work, I was told to behave in a certain professional way. I have an upbeat personality and a loud laugh. My manager said that others could perceive me as not intelligent. He said that perception is everything and if I wanted to be treated with respect, I needed to behave less bubbly. This way was rigid and without personality and I listened and took on his belief. I believed that I had to do and say the right thing otherwise I would get fired. I couldn't relax and just be myself. As I progressed in my career and in my maturity, I realized that this was a false belief that I had learned. Therefore, I didn't need to follow this rigid way of thinking. Of course, I remained professional but added my own personality back into the mix. I began to make more jokes, share about my personal life, and enjoy work more. By being me, I was able to build stronger relationships with my co-workers.

As I mentioned before, your core self will not betray you. You know what is okay to say to others without jeopardizing yourself. By being real, I was humble. When I was less bubbly, I was not my genuine self. Instead, this may have been portrayed as being unauthentic. When someone is perceived this way, it is hard to build sustaining relationships. Instead, I needed to come from a place of authenticity and love, which is humbleness.

Many believe in the constructs of this world and that to be accepted only particular behavior is acceptable. This isn't necessarily a bad thing but something to be aware of. For example, children are taught to be polite and have manners. In other words, it is right to censor your thoughts and words as to not hurt anyone's feelings. Or that particular clothing is acceptable to look professional. Or that certain words are "bad" and shouldn't be used in public.

Who would you be if you didn't have these beliefs? Would you be different and seen more as an individual than like everyone else? These views give a false message that who you are at your core isn't good enough. It is saying that you can't trust yourself to know what is best for you and for society. You must listen to what your mother/father and all of your teachers have said you must be. What if, instead, you looked inside to know? Inside everyone is an inner knowing that recognizes what is best.

The more experiences I have, the more I realize that being me is the best thing. Discarding the beliefs that have been programmed into me is actually fruitful. As just mentioned, I have been told I have a big personality. In my profession as an Electrical Engineer, I have stifled that because a manager told me that I should. What I've noticed is that my big personality has actually strengthened my relationships. People enjoy it when I am genuine. Even though my manager told me to do this and I listened, it was still hard to completely cover up who I was. When my authenticity came out, others around me smiled, laughed, and enjoyed my company. Humans are not robots; every person has a unique part in this world. This individuality is needed to add variety to life. Humility is the path to seeing who we really are at our roots.

Another pure quality mantra is this: *We are all created equal, but different; we all have strengths and weaknesses.*

You may be an excellent driver but horrible with cooking; while I may be an exceptional chef and an awful driver. Who am I to say I am better than you because of certain talents and abilities that I have versus what you have? In some of my college classes, some of my classmates thrived while I struggled. In other classes, I succeeded while some of them struggled. We all had our strengths and weaknesses in various subjects.

I would get down on myself because I wasn't getting the material as well as my peers in these particular subjects. It would have been a benefit to know that everyone has strengths and weaknesses. Focusing on my gifts would have been better. Even with our various talents in particular subjects, it turns out that we all graduated with the same degree and got excellent jobs.

Personally, I discovered that my soft skills were great and above the typical engineer compared to my peers. I learned that we are not all the same (How boring would that be?) but that we are all very different. Everyone has various talents and abilities, so there is no need to be down on yourself for not having something that someone else has. Whenever I feel down about my ability in a particular area, I remember that I have strengths in other capacities, just as it was intended for me.

My husband, Nate, happens to be excellent at knowing how things work and other factoids. At first, I thought this was amazing and admired his vast range of knowledge.

After a few months, I began to think it was not so cute. He knew everything! I resisted what he had to say and we would argue for lengths at a time. I don't want to admit this, but almost every time I would look something up that we were fighting over, he was correct. Darn! I wasn't very humble. Instead, I was resisting being taught new things for the sake of wanting to be right (or, at least, I thought I was right). As I practiced being humble, I learned that it was okay to listen, to be open and to learn from Nate. He had many valuable insights from science and politics to relationships. Further, he had surprised me many times by giving me insights about love and relationships. By being open and humble, I was able to learn more than I thought possible.

Creating a space for learning is being humble. Know that opening yourself up to other people's knowledge can be beneficial. Allowing yourself to be present will open up the possibilities for you to flourish. It's the kindness that you have toward yourself and others that will deepen your relationships and bring you closer. This pure quality of being humble is a way to get to that space.

Another way of showing your humility is to serve others. This does not include being walked all over or being taken advantage of. You still need to have boundaries. However, serving is an exceptional way to dip your feet in the water. When you serve, you are going out of your way to help someone else; you are thinking about their needs. Serving feels great; it has this natural positive feeling effect.

In your most precious relationship, how do you serve? Do you go out of your way to make this person feel special? At home, I enjoy preparing Nate's coffee the night before so it is ready when he wakes up. To go the extra step, with love, I make sure to use filtered water and that the reusable coffee filter is cleaned and dried from the day before as to not expose him to any germs. By doing this, I feel good and I hope he does too. There are many other ways to serve your loved one. This doesn't mean you are a slave, as it should come from a place of love and enjoyment and at your own will.

Most of us function from a place of good intentions. When a stranger opens a door for you, he is serving you. When your friend picks you up and takes you out to lunch, she is serving you. Your sister surprises you by coming over to clean your house; this is a gift in the form of serving. There are an abundant amount of ways to serve others. Look for these favors in every moment. You will be rewarded abundantly.

Besides doing for others, take note of what others do for you. Nate lays out his clothes every night in the living room so he doesn't disturb me by turning the lights on in the morning. My friend goes into work later than his wife; he could sleep in, but instead he wakes up at the same time and makes her coffee and breakfast. He is serving her with love and they have a beautiful relationship. What does your loved one do for you? Have you noticed how it puts a smile on his or her face? Serving each other is a beautiful gift.

I host several parties a year, and I enjoy every minute of it. There is a lot of preparation and serving, but it's worth it. I get to enjoy the company of my friends as they drink and eat the food I have prepared for them. In the end, they are grateful, and our friendship is deepened even more. This is a gift for them and me. So, the next time you hear that someone needs a glass of water or help with a project at work, volunteer to help. If you feel good afterward, serve again.

Let's go one step further and apply this toward yourself. How could you serve yourself more? As I put lotion on my legs every morning, I take the time to massage it into my skin. I tell my legs that I love them and how grateful I am to have them. They do so much for me. I could just slather the lotion on, but I take the extra time to honor myself; which makes me feel good. Serving yourself means being loving to you. It means doing what you would do for others, for yourself. We can get in the habit of giving to everyone else and forgetting about ourselves.

Self-love is just as important as outward love; both mirror each other. If you are giving love, you will receive love. This love won't necessarily come from the place you gave love to; however, the power of love is always in motion. When you give love, it will be returned and it may come from the most unexpected places.

On my train ride to work, I would practice giving love to others around me by smiling and not pushing my way onto the train. In return, a train attendant, Cheryl, had a seat saved for me. It's not to say that she knew of my acts of love but the Universe delivered. It's possible that Cheryl saw me smiling the days before and thought of me as someone she would like to do this for. We didn't know each other, but when I walked by, she offered me the seat she was in and said she saved it for me. She had a big smile and I could feel her affection. This was an unexpected gift of love.

Serving is best done with love. It is the love behind it that makes it so powerful. A wife could do many tasks around the house for her husband, but without love, they

35

are just actions. Instead of just doing the laundry she separates her husband's dress shirts and washes them on a gentle cycle. She does this because she wants her husband to enjoy wearing his well-taken care of dress shirts. She could just wash them on the normal cycle but they may not come out as nicely. Through love, she is performing this act. It is a win-win for both, she feels good about showing her love and he feels good about receiving her love.

Any action with love behind it has the influence to change the energy surrounding it. For example, opening a door for an elderly person is a kind thing to do and it will most likely be appreciated, but opening it with love and a smile will speak volumes. Most likely the positive energy will carry into the day or night ahead for yourself and that person. How much better would your world be if you did everything with love? It is the prevailing force behind every wonderful outcome.

As you begin to practice humility, notice your thoughts about others. The world teaches to look at the differences between others and yourself. It says to compare and contrast and judge what is better or worse. This act of judgment is detrimental to the spirit of love. It is only negating and separating you from others. When in reality, everyone is connected and on this journey together.

Have you ever noticed the similarities between you and someone you just met? Everyone has something physical that they struggle with. Each and every person has issues that they must deal with every day. These physical struggles may be different, but the underlying struggle is the same. A person dealing with being overweight and another dealing with believing they're unattractive still has to learn self-love. Their thoughts are similar, *I dislike my body* or *I hate how I look.* Or you may see a person in a wheelchair and think you have nothing in common with them. Therefore, you keep your distance and lose out on meeting a great person. It is easy to quickly judge because someone looks different. The ailment is the only thing that is seen and judgment takes place based on that difference. This is what is taught. Being slow to critic is the ability to see that everyone has something that they are dealing with. Everyone needs kindness and love. This is the ego wanting to feel good and be the best, above everyone else. However, is any person really above anyone else?

The act of humility is non-judgment. It is recognizing that you have been that person sitting in the room speaking obnoxiously loud. You've been the person to cut someone off in traffic. There have been times when you've been so upset that you've caused a scene. This human experience is similar for all. Needless to say, the details of the stories are different, but the underlying lessons are the same. You are here to learn about self-love. This is the key lesson because by loving yourself, you can love others. It is a cycle of endless love, and this love requires being humble and non-judgmental toward others.

When I lived in California and commuted on public transit, one of the gifts was meeting people I usually would not have encountered. I became friends with one lady easily; we talked the whole ride home for an hour, we had many similarities. As our conversation progressed, she thought of a way she could help me with my cyber security job. She was in charge of running cyber security gatherings for professionals in the Bay Area. She knew that I was in this field and invited me to a few events. From those two events, I made great contacts. Just by being open and in non-judgment to a stranger, and resonating openness and love, I made an incredible connection. She connected me with people that were a good fit for my professional career (as well as good friends now, too). In turn, I invited her into my circle of friends. This friendship was mutually beneficial, and it all happened because we were both humble and open.

Another lady I met was very kind and easy to speak with. We also had many similarities. All it took was, "Hi, how are you?" and she opened up and we had a great conversation.

From her, I learned that it was okay not to work in the profession related to your college degree. That exploring outside of it is acceptable and better if one is happier doing something else. She had a master's degree in Computer Science; however, she was in product marketing. She said it was more interesting to her.

Regardless of people's differences, whether they are physical, spiritual, or cultural, everyone has fears, anxieties, enjoyments, and love. Every person looks different because of their height, weight, eye color, etc. Does that mean that they are better or less than each other? Of course not; they are just physically different.

People judge each other on many various aspects such as the car someone drives, the clothes somebody wears, individual food choices, weight, or religion. The fact is that it is impossible to know what is going on inside of anyone. As you get to know someone, you will see the similarities of love, compassion, and the desire of self-discovery. Every person has the aspiration to reach self-love, whether they know it yet or not. That is the purpose of this life.

Give a smile, hand, or gift to a stranger. They will most likely be humbled by your generosity. And in turn, you will be humbled knowing that you can affect someone this way. Life is so beautiful that you can have that type of impact on someone; it's that easy.

As you begin to meet new people, practice listening to others without judgment. Understand that you could be in someone else's shoes at some point. Give your compassion and love for them and their situation. Being humble is about seeing the equality of the human race. It is about serving each other with love.

COUNSEL

*Love counsels; it shares
wise advice and listens.*

*C*ounseling requires deep compassion for the other person. Have you ever talked to someone about a problem and it felt like they just didn't care? Did you take their advice seriously or did you dismiss it because it seemed insincere? The truth is that to give good counsel, you need to have compassion for the person and their situation. All humans are going through the same human condition and are, therefore, able to understand through empathy what the other person is going through. Compassion comes from a place of deep understanding and love. When you can understand a situation, then you can give good counsel to a friend.

Love counsels with compassion and understanding. It is able to help a friend in need. Love knows to be gentle when giving guidance to others. Being gentle allows non-resistance to exist; therefore, the person can hear what you are saying. It is also able to listen without interruption to what the person is saying. In this way, you can come to the best understanding of the situation. Love also knows to ask questions to bring light to the situation where there is darkness. As a compilation of all of the pure qualities, love is able to give wise counsel to others.

My sister gave me counsel on a matter concerning my mother. I was back in Colorado from California, where my mom lives, to visit friends over the weekend and I didn't take the time to see my mom. After I was back in California, talking on the phone with my sister, she mentioned that I should have taken the time to see her. When she brought this up, of course, I felt sorry but I didn't let my sister know. Instead, I resisted what she said and defended why I didn't have time. The trip was to visit friends and I had seen my mom two weeks prior. I didn't want to hear her advice. Looking back, she meant it with love—love for me and love for my mom.

Feeling guilty, I tried to justify my actions. After some time, I apologized to my mom and realized that I should have taken the time to see her. This would have been honoring our relationship. My sister's advice took some time to acknowledge and come to terms with. That is okay. In the beginning, her help was not sought after but it turned out to be valuable.

If a friend has some advice that is hard to hear, listen, and take the time to think about it. What is best for you and your situation? What makes you feel light and comfortable? Follow the advice that is right for you. The answer is within you.

The people around you are constantly giving you signs and messages of advice. Have you ever asked a question and then there were signs guiding your path? The easiest sign to see is an open or closed door. A road that has minimum to zero barriers is the path that is the most desirable. When this happens, it is because your desire was heard and a path illuminated for you to effortlessly follow. Life is meant to be that easy. It is only ourselves that get in the way. You have the choice to choose, and if you want to see the open door and walk through it, it will bring about the results you desire.

Have you ever tried to accomplish something but it just wasn't working? This is a closed door. On the other hand, have you put a desire out there and then *bam!* it happened without even trying? That is an open door. Allowing these open doors to direct your life will bring ease to your spirit. Additionally, you can trust that there is always an open door for you.

An open door could be as simple as your friend making a comment about a decision that you have been contemplating. I was at dinner with a group of friends and one of them mentioned how unstable a start-up business can be compared to an established business. I'm not sure how we got on this topic but I didn't bring it up. It just so happened that I was contemplating whether to take a job with a start-up or an established company. The main thing that I wanted at the time was stability. When he made his comment, it instantly struck a chord with me. I knew it was a sign and an invitation to walk through the open door. I decided to take a job with the established company because what I mainly wanted was stability.

Communicating, listening, and sharing are the essential ingredients for creating a connection in a relationship. As the well-known American psychiatrist, Karl Menninger said, "Listening is a magnetic and strange thing, a creative force. The friends who listen to us are the ones we move toward. When we are listened to, it creates us, makes us unfold" (Menninger, 1893-1990).

Building relationships encompasses actively listening to one another. Everybody has wants, desires, and struggles. When there is compassion for one another's situations, then they can be worked through together. Since everyone has these needs, try to listen to others without judgment; doing so will create a welcoming space to open up. Also, it helps you to be honest about your feelings.

What's more, life requires feedback. It is important to let the other person know you are hearing what she is saying. It's easy to insert your own opinions and feelings; however, stay in non-judgment so she can find what is truly right for her. Ask questions to guide her to a decision that she is comfortable with and that is true for her. Questions open up possibilities that she may not have thought about. Then, give her the time to reflect and answer back.

It is important to remember to give advice carefully and to receive counsel from a trusted source. As the famed late comedian Joan Rivers said, "Don't follow any advice, no matter how good, until you feel as deeply in your spirit as you think in your mind that the counsel is wise" (Rivers, 1933-2014).

Advice should be taken with discretion and from a trusted source. Ultimately, you should think through any counsel to where it is right with you. Ask yourself the following question, *When I hear this advice, does it feel light and sit well with me, or does it feel heavy?* Follow your knowing and trust the lightness of what feels right for you. Then, take action of the guidance that is accurate for you; learn and grow. Receive advice that is love-driven, and counsel others with love.

I have two great mothers: my mom, Pina, and my mother-in-law, Alanna. They both have wise counsel and superb advice whenever I need it. There were several months where I was unemployed. My husband got a job with Facebook in California where we decided to uproot our lives in Colorado and move west. As an Electrical Engineer in the data storage industry, I was confident that I would find a job quickly and easily. This was not the case. That time was different than I had imagined. Thankfully, I was in school getting my masters in Engineering Management to keep me busy which gave me the opportunity to focus on my studies. Needless to say, it wasn't without its perfect lessons. I am grateful my mothers were there to help me through it.

Both advised me to enjoy the time, practice patience and be grateful. My mom taught me to be grateful for what I had at that moment. Enjoying all that I had right then was her wise counsel for me. She guided me to take notice of everything that I did have: a beautiful apartment, sunny days, new friends, and new places to explore. The beauty of her advice was that it was precisely the wise counsel that I needed to hear. It was without judgment or her opinion of what I should be doing.

Focusing on the beauty of that present moment was the gift handed to me. In that time, it seemed hard to understand why I had not gotten a job in the high-tech industry. Especially since I was in the middle of Silicon Valley where high-tech jobs were in abundance. However, deep inside of me, I did understand. There was a higher power at work.

I had asked many questions to guide me to that point in my life. My passion for teaching others about love was strong. During that time, I had additional time to read and write about what love is. If I had a full-time job, I wouldn't have had that time.

The wise advice from my mother-in-law, Alanna, involved focusing on the positive things going on in my life and to just be. This act of being is profound because that is all that really exists. The future that I had created in my mind didn't exist in that reality. I had thought I would find a job quickly and love living in California. My reality looked much different. There was nothing wrong with what I'd experienced, and there was a reason for it. It was a reason that I didn't quite understand yet. Alanna explained that I should enjoy that time in my life as much as possible. She was very insightful and suggested that I write down all the things that were fun for me.

My list:

Reading and writing

Spending time with my family and friends

Travelling to unique places

Trying new restaurants with friends

Visiting art museums

As Alanna encouraged me to write down things that I thought were fun I invite you to do the same thing. Be open to what you write down as enjoyable, and let this awareness sit with you. Focusing on these pleasurable things will steer you in that direction.

Having an awareness and being open to new possibilities is the first step in creating the life you desire. For me, just sitting here and writing I know that this is one activity that I love to do. I love to connect and bring people together, which is more possible when the pure qualities are practiced. This is my passion. The gift in me not having a job during that time was that I was able to explore what I truly loved to do. My mother-in-law's counsel was wise. It felt light and right for me.

Speaking about creating the life you desire and wise counsel, a group of my friends and I have an ongoing group text. My sweet friend started it with a few of our girlfriends. She had a wise word to share with us. She shared with us a question, "What sparks your joy?"

Since then I have been asking this question throughout my day. It has led me to choose and think differently. Instead of going to my normal gym this week, I went to a new yoga studio because it sparked joy in me. I am so glad I went because it was exactly the peaceful space that my spirit needed at that time. Another time, when I was waiting in line at the store, feeling bored, I asked this question. My answer was that I am sparked with joy when I think about travel. From there I started daydreaming about going to Scotland. Instantly, my joy was sparked and my boredom diminished as I was distracted by the new idea. I went home and started researching Scotland. I don't have any definite plans yet, but it was and is exciting to think about it.

By my friend sharing her wise counsel in the form of this question, my week was enhanced. Lastly, having a group text with my close girlfriends was inspirational as we shared support and counsel with each other. Create your own inspirational and active group text message with your friends and see what wise counsel comes your way.

When you find yourself in a situation and need advice, seek it from those you trust. Only receive wise advice that feels right to you. Inside you will know what the best thing for you to do is. Listen to that inner knowing and voice within you.

Patience

*Love is patient; it waits
without complaint*

$\mathcal{P}$atience is a pure quality that is developed through experiences. If I didn't have the experience of road rage that almost got me in a car accident, then I probably wouldn't be as patient as I am now on the road. When others zoom past me or cut me off, I am much more relaxed and patient, knowing that I don't want to get into a road rage incident.

Patience is a construct of the spiritual world. It is within you when you choose it. Each encounter in life gives you the opportunity to grow in patience. Have you ever noticed one specific issue that kept coming up in your life? Then, suddenly it was gone. For example, it may have been seeing crying babies everywhere. Their screaming sound pierced your ears and you became irritated while others around you may not even have noticed the crying babies. This was a lesson especially for you. This was your opportunity to choose to be patient and to have a different understanding that the baby is just like how you were when you were a child. With this understanding, you became compassionate. You began to grow patience with your compassion. Eventually, you didn't hear screaming babies anymore because you had learned to be patient and understanding. Lesson was learned.

Building patience is important because as it builds, so does your spiritual growth. Patience can be taught in many different ways and at different levels. As your strength improves, you are able to handle certain situations better. For example, at a higher standard of patience, you will be more tolerant of your manager's complaining. His manager may notice your increased tolerance. One day you may get a promotion because of your noticed patience with your boss. Spiritually you are on a higher path, which brings greater rewards into your life. Your reward is handed to you because you have learned patience with other things. You were open and received the lesson of patience (i.e., with the screaming baby) and are therefore able to be patient in other aspects of your life that affect you positively.

A way to practice patience is to not complain. The act of complaining is conflicting; it brings others and yourself down. Complaints hurt relationships because they are based on self-preservation. In other words, you are thinking about yourself only. It doesn't include the needs and desires of others.

Let's say you and two other girlfriends are going to meet up for lunch. Your friend Lucy shows up on time.

Laura is running late so you complain to Lucy about Laura being late. As you share your feelings with Lucy, she begins to think about a time she was late before. She now sees what you think about people who are late; that this is a great annoyance to you. She's thinking, *I've been late before when my mom really needed to talk to me on the phone.*

As you complain about your unpunctual friend Laura, your other relationship is hurt. Instead, practice patience and have compassion for your late friend. Most likely she has a good reason for being late, and if she doesn't, still have compassion. Due to her lateness, you were able to build the extraordinary quality of patience. Also, you were able to have one-on-one time with Lucy. Two bonuses! This is the pure quality way.

In life, some situations cannot be explained at the time. There is a divine order that you are unable to see. In this space, practice being present. In other words, focus on the now instead of the past or future. By being present, you are practicing patience. When you are patient, the Universe will deliver what you desire. Trust in this powerful essence to guide you.

Many times we want what we want now; however, forcing something into fruition is hard and it doesn't work. It also may not show up as good as it could have been when it is forced. For example, Kim was looking for a new job opportunity. She thought she understood what it was she wanted: high profile, lucrative, and fast-paced. Kim had this notion of the perfect job. Willingly, she spent a lot of effort into attaining this ideal situation. Once, Kim found a job opening that matched her criteria she spent copious amounts of time, energy, and worry. In the end, she did not get the job. She worried and worked hard, trying to force the situation to occur.

After her loss, she gave up. Little did she know, that her ideal situation was coming to her. A friend who knew of Kim's circumstances had put in a good word with her manager. The position was not only ideal for Kim but it had additional bonuses that she had not thought of. She was grateful in the end that she did not get the other job but landed this one. The lesson for her was to let go and not force the doors open. The doors will open with ease when the Universe is involved. How many times have you pushed a door open realizing later that an open door was heading your way without any worry? Life is easy. Be present for it, and you won't miss the open doors.

Patience is learned as you practice it. Building patience is an advantage and will contribute to every aspect of your life. As your life unfolds, it is the key to enjoying it to its full potential. Rushing around and not noticing the very precious moment that you have is the opposite of being present. Practice noticing everything around you. Do you see the magnificence of your body? Of nature? Of your friends and family? As you begin to notice the treasures around you, can you feel your excitement building? As the love for life grows inside of you, this is when you are truly open to the abundance of the Universe. It is only by being present and patient can you begin to receive the love that is available to you.

This acknowledgment of the present moment, instead of thinking about the future or the past, is the fulfilling of your heart. Begin practicing being patient with everyone and everything. The entire Universe is speaking to you. It has a message for you and it's the very message that your soul desires to hear. Push back the chatter of your mind and take note of what is around you. The benefit of patience is abundant. The best part is how happy life will become when you practice patience and presence.

Most of the best opportunities occur when least expected. Jill is a very present woman. She works diligently for her company and always with a smile. One day her manager told her that she was being promoted to a new group and a new role. She had asked the Universe for something better months before. She had patience and did not force the issue. In other words, she didn't start a full-time job search as Kim had. With patience, love, and acceptance she continued with her current job, trusting. A few months went by, and in some people's minds, that is too long. For Jill, though, by being patient and waiting those few months she got a great job offer without even trying. In other words, she asked the Universe and waited for the open door.

The door opened for her without difficulty. The point is not to do anything; it is to ask the Universe, be your best self, and let it go by trusting that you have been heard. If she would have forced the issue and found a new job, it may not have been as good as the one that just came to her with ease. Life is stress-free if you just allow the natural timing of it. Letting your heart's desire be known to the Universe, being present, and waiting patiently is the easier way. This universal force is pure love and it wants to give you your desire. It will come naturally in the perfect timing of the Universe.

You were born with many unique talents to share with the world. Through love and with love you can share the gifts that you were born with. Noticing your surroundings, giving love to those around you, making space for the magic of the Universe; this is what you are here to experience. Allow the moment of today to lead you on your path. Have you ever noticed that big changes occur when you least expect them? This is the divine creating magic for you. A promotion, a baby, an inheritance, a new girlfriend, boyfriend, or hobby comes into your life at a surprising time is an unexpected blessing of love.

Having patience isn't an easy task. It takes conscious effort, but the rewards will far outweigh the effort. There are many ways to practice patience such as by being present. Literally, notice your breath and how it can function without your conscious help, yet it's vital to live. Look at your fingers—what a gift! Every part of your body is intricately made for your pleasure. Take notice and be grateful for every part of it. Be aware of the people around you. They are contributing to your environment. If they weren't there, would you miss their energy? Notice the chair you're sitting on—is there anything interesting about it? Someone (or a machine that a man made) made that. They designed and created it with their unique talent. You get to enjoy their ability that they are sharing with the world.

By being present, you will notice the beauty that is all around you and that is exciting! Perhaps, instead of gray walls, there are bright yellow walls with pictures of art hanging on them for your pleasure. Notice the gift of electricity. Light gives humans the ability to see in the dark. Further, humans have created aesthetically eye-catching, decorated fixtures for pure enjoyment. How awe-inspiring that is! As you begin to see all the gifts around you, can you feel your energy lift? In this moment, are you thinking about the past or future? Not at all, instead, you are in the present, taking in all the exceptional talents that others are sharing. These pleasing things are always here for you, waiting for you to take notice. Life is not how you make it; it is how you see it.

As you become aware of your surroundings, see all the good in your life. Feel grateful for all that you have instead of what you don't have. There is a reason you don't have some things. You may not know what that reason is, and that's okay. Good things are working on your behalf. The power that you have when you are present is vast. At that moment, you can be within the spirit of gratefulness, which is a powerful force. By stirring up the feelings of gratefulness within you, you are creating more good things into your life. This can only happen when you are present. If you are thinking about how you would like to lose ten pounds and then you will be happy, then you're not noticing the beauty of your body right now. When you think about a past hurtful breakup, you are not able to see the beauty of a potential mate right in front of you. The power of being present is the answer to the beautiful life you desire.

Expanding on your love capability requires patience. Love is the catalyst that keeps your life running beautifully. It is the power of presence and patience and it is such a beautiful notion. As you are in acceptance of the Universe's timing, it will shower you back with love. It knows what you require. It also likes to hear from you. If you desire to experience a warm, sunny beach, then tell it. You don't need to force the issue by booking a ticket to Mexico. Wait and let the Universe present the beach to you. This is probably a very different approach than you are used to. However, it will answer and it will look different than you thought. Instead of Mexico, the Universe will go a step further. It may open a door for you to go to an exotic beach on a Hawaiian island on a private yacht. If the Universe created you and the nature that surrounds you, how much more are its gifts for you?

The amazing part of gratitude is that it is so easy to access its power. In your thoughts and words, you can speak your gratitude. As you do this, you will feel the lightness. Expressing your gratitude is fun. It will bring the feeling of contentment and it connects you. When you are connected, then you are in alignment. Being in alignment means that you are able to receive all the possible gifts for you. Even more, there is no need to worry about anything because being grateful brings you to the present moment. At that moment, there is no past or future so there are no worries. Voicing your gratitude for everything is your choice and if you choose to do it, be aware of what good comes into your life.

To practice this powerful tool when you wake up in the morning, name two things you are grateful for. And just when you are about to fall asleep, name another two things that you are grateful for. Besides this, anytime is a good time to express your gratefulness, such as in the shower, brushing your teeth, cooking dinner, driving, or talking to a friend.

My mother and I were discussing gratitude. She has a rental property business that can be stressful at times. For many years, she has labored with challenging occupants. She does her best to deal with the situation at hand. However, this year she decided to have deep gratitude for everything that came her way including these occupants.

As she practiced being grateful, things turned around within days. These tenants began to apologize and admit that they were in the wrong. They didn't argue with her anymore. All she did was put herself into a state of gratitude. This focused her attention on what was going well for her instead of what wasn't. As she did this, her world changed to magnify what she had been concentrating on. She had the choice and accessed this within herself. There are unlimited opportunities to express your gratefulness as she did. The possibilities are waiting to be discovered and given to you. Align yourself and see what changes occur in your life.

Another method to become present is to take a walk in nature. It's in nature where everything is present. The birds aren't thinking about the meal they had last night; no, they are singing to the sun for the beautiful day. The grass isn't wilting because winter will be here in three months. No, it's alive and green as it should be at that moment. Take off your shoes and feel the grass beneath your feet. Can you feel its energy rise up within you? Get close to a flower and notice all of its details. As you are present, there are no other problems because there is no space to think about the future (which hasn't happened yet) or the past (which has already occurred). The beauty of the flower is a gift for you to enjoy right now and to feed your spirit with love.

The famous "Love Chapter" in the Bible starts off with "Love is patient..." (Holy Bible N. I., Bible Gateway, 1 Cor. 13:4). The Bible directly tells us that a quality of love is patience. Or in other words, being patient is love. As humans, we need to give and receive love. It's part of our nature and survival to have relationships that include love.

This timeless quality unites people. Without patience, relationships would be hopeless. Since we are all unique beings and come from different perspectives, we need to be able to be patient with each other as we journey through this life together.

Your patience will be tested many times. Imagine you are on vacation with your mother and father. Their schedule and needs are probably different than yours. While you have a need for breakfast early in the morning, they may need extra sleep. This could be a conflict if you want to stick together. One must be patient for the other as personal needs are fulfilled.

Recently, my husband and I went on a trip to New Zealand with our good friends. As travel companions, we got along great. We had very similar needs and desires. That being said, there were a few times when one person or a couple had different needs than the rest of the group. This was when patience was required. Throughout the whole trip, at least, every person in the group needed something that the others didn't. Either I needed to find a restroom or my friend needed to sit in the front seat so she wouldn't get carsick. Each of these situations took love, compassion, and patience. What situations have you had to be patient for and vice versa, others being patient with you? It is a perfect exchange of love.

Life is colorful. There are so many places, people, and things to explore. By having patience in all that you do, you will discover that situations can change quickly. By putting questions out there and waiting patiently, new opportunities will come to you. Therefore, enjoy this point in your life. Explore the gifts in what you are experiencing right now. If you have a job that you don't like too much, ask yourself what you do like about it. Focus on that. You will notice that by focusing on the positive, more of that goodness will come to you. It's the law of the Universe, a.k.a. The Law of Attraction—"Like attracts like" (Contributors, 2016). In other words, you will attract more of what you focus on.

Have you been told that you have to make your life happen; it's not going to happen to you? Doesn't that sound hard, trying to make your life happen? Instead, consider a different way. Life is not how you make it; it is how you see it. Your perception is your choice. An easy example is to consider working out your body for health as opposed to losing weight. Isn't it more motivating to work out for more energy and a long, healthy life to spend with your friends and family? The thought of working out for weight loss feels like a burden. It is only your perception that can change the way a situation looks for you.

Having patience in your daily life will be a benefit to all that you do. Watch what happens. When standing in line for coffee, practice being patient. Notice the people around you, sitting down or in line. Maybe smile at them or ask them how their day is. It's interesting what information you will come across by being present and patient in line at a coffee shop. I once met a woman that brightened my whole day by having a two-minute conversation with her. She told me about a friend she was going to visit in New York and how long it had been since she had seen her. This sparked me to call my friend in New York. It turned out that my friend needed someone to talk to. I am glad that I was able to be there for her. That sequence of events wouldn't have happened if I didn't speak to the lady in line at the coffee shop. What a powerful sequence of events from just being patient and present. My friend was grateful that I called. Ultimately, I was grateful for that reminder from the Universe to call her.

All of these pure qualities are intertwined and they all require love. They teach love. By being patient, I smiled at the person in front of me in line. If I had been impatient, I would not have made eye contact with anyone. I would have had bad energy and missed my opportunity to connect with my friend. I would have been rude to the barista, which could have put him in a bad mood. This could have affected the next person if that barista decided to let my impatience affect him. The domino effect would have taken place. We are all connected. Spreading patience, a positive attitude, and love for everyone are several of the gifts you have to share. Not only will you be a gift to others but you will also be gifted back.

TRUST

*Love is trusting; it keeps its
word and follows through.*

hat is trust? Is there more than one definition? Does it mean something different to one person than to another? If you were to Google *trust,* you would find many definitions. According to Merriam-Webster trust is defined as, "A reliance on the character, ability, strength, or truth of someone or something," and "One in which confidence is placed" (Trust, 2016).

This five-letter word - *trust* - is possibly one of the hardest things to do. It is the one word that is so crucial to great relationships. It is trust between two people that creates a bond that enables a relationship to exist. Without trust, it is difficult to sustain any relationship as it is the glue that binds two people together. Trust takes time to build. It is developed through experiences. Unfortunately, it takes even less time to break a relationship. Further, current relationships can be affected by past relationships that had "trust issues." This is a vital quality that is required for any relationship to flourish; however, it is such a sensitive subject.

How is trust built? Initially, between two people, when they first meet, there is no trust. Or there may be a small amount depending on your past experiences. For example, when you meet another person through a friend there may be more trust initially than meeting a stranger on the street. However, trust still needs to be built through experiences and conversation.

Each event that one shares together builds trust among a relationship. Every conversation, where you find similarities between each other, also builds confidence in each other. Finding things in common makes one feel closer to another through these mutual occurrences. For example, Jason meets Steve for the first time in his kickball league. While waiting for their turn to the plate, they are getting to know each other. They learn that they both live in downtown and have high-tech jobs. After learning this information, they feel they can trust each other to a certain level because they have these things in common. Jason decides to invite Steve out for drinks with his friends after the game. He feels safe (or trust) with Steve to at least invite him out. This is the first initial build-up of confidence among two people based on similarities.

Furthermore, trust is built over time and with experiences. Fast forward with Jason and Steve; they have been playing for the kickball team for a full season now. They have become quick friends and enjoy hanging out together. When on the field they have each other's backs, catching balls and encouraging each other. One day Steve wasn't paying attention to the field and almost got hit by the ball. Jason was there before it hit Steve in the face. This one act built, even more, trust from Jason to Steve that he can count on him.

The growth of trust is a process over time. It is an enduring quality and can only be genuine if there is love backing it up. There are many dimensions to this timeless quality. It is the basis for all high-quality relationships. The act of trust and being trustworthy are a necessity for any authentic relationship to develop.

Besides trust in your relationships, trust in the Universe, or your higher source, this is also imperative. When I forget to trust the Universe, I simply lose control of who I am. I become distant and unkind to myself and to others around me. I feel lost when I am not in trust. When this happens, I need to remind myself to trust in the Universe and practice the pure qualities.

Watch and take note; when you are feeling distant and angry, are you trusting the Universe? It is everywhere to guide you with its soft, steady, calm voice. Know that you can trust it and allow it to guide you to where you want to go. Ultimately, the place we are all attempting to reach is inner peace, happiness, and self-love. This is where we actually feel at home with the Universe, our friends, family, and ourselves.

One way to build confidence and become more trustworthy is to keep your word and follow through. If you say that you are going to clean up your mess around the house tonight, then do it. Your partner will feel more confident in your word and, therefore, feel you are more trustworthy. When this confidence grows, it will also progress in the larger things.

Here is a story about a man and a woman who experience infidelity. For this example, Jacob cheats on Melissa. Melissa feels betrayed and feels she cannot trust Jacob ever again. She trusted Jacob. He feels truly sorry and asks for forgiveness many times as he wants to rebuild his relationship with Melissa. After many hard conversations, Melissa decides to work things out. However, it could take years before Melissa feels she can trust Jacob again. The only way to build that confidence again is if Jacob follows through with his word. If he says he will be out bowling with his guy friends and Melissa sees that he is doing that, then her confidence in him will grow. This repetitious act will build trust back in their relationship.

Having trust in any relationship can be difficult when you've been bruised in the past. Memories of the past remind us of how we were hurt. In this way, it keeps us stuck in the past and never moving forward with the here and now. The current situation that you are in with your boyfriend, mother, father, or friend is what is happening right now. The past is a former self, someone who had a different outlook on life. Your perspective was based upon all of your other experiences. Basically, you were different and whatever relationship you are in now doesn't need to be based on a past time in your life.

Memories are two-fold. It is a blessing to remember certain aspects of your life and, on the other hand, a difficulty as you may want to forget certain pieces. Memories of being with family, spending time with friends in school, and your 21st birthday are all experiences to remember;

as well as bad relationships and bitter breakups. All of these times allow you to reflect and change if you want to. On the contrary, some memories can keep you stuck in the past.

If you went through a bad break-up, you might have said you will never go through that again. Consequently, you are afraid to go through another bad break-up and, therefore, stay in a harmful relationship. Or you may have been with a man who didn't compliment you enough and so you said you will never be with a man who doesn't give out compliments. Yet, you may be missing out on a wonderful man because he's not good at complimenting, but he's good at many other things. All of these judgments and conclusions only keep you stuck in the past instead of rising to the present moment. This is the only moment you actually have. Why base it on your past experiences. Is that really fair? Is this really a good way to look at current life situations?

How many times have you been judged based on something in the past that you did? Did you think that was unfair because you have changed? My friend Elizabeth is a strong, independent woman. She has always taken care of her own needs and she is proud of that. She got into a relationship with John and this is one of the things he loves about her. As their relationship progressed and John proposed, she realized that she would like to combine their checking accounts. This was a huge step for Elizabeth to even ask or to even consider. She's always thought of her money as hers and John's as his. However, she was ready to become more combined financially. At first, John was resistant. He said, "When I first met you, this was something that you said you never wanted to do.

You stated that you wanted to keep your independence. That is something that I love about you."

Elizabeth didn't back down and explained to John that she still is independent and she thinks this is the next natural step now that they are engaged. Especially, since they already share many financial burdens together. His judgment was clouded by how he perceived her in the past. Elizabeth was allowed to change. This is the consequence in judging others—it keeps us stuck. Eventually, John was able to remove his long-standing judgment of Elizabeth. He accepted this new part of her. The point is that we all change. Being stuck in past experiences doesn't align one with the current situation and ultimately, doesn't contribute to the relationship.

To honor others by sharing your real self, you must learn to be present. It's one of the universal keys to your happiness. Being present completely requires you to not have judgments or conclusions from the past nor be worried or anxious about the future. It is enjoying this very moment as you read these words from this book. It is being completely aware of how you are feeling at this moment as you are. It is void of anxious thoughts about the future.

There is no need to worry when you are present because the future hasn't even happened yet. Be aware of what you would like to manifest in the future by focusing on what you would like to manifest now. Once again, it is The Law of Attraction; be and feel what you desire now and it will attract more of that in the future. It's simple.

To be present takes practice. It's easy to get caught up with the everyday woes and business of life. Having been in the corporate world for 10 years, I have experienced first-hand getting caught up in all the stresses of daily business. At times like these, it's easy to be consumed by the problems of the day. This can lead to a lot of stress. Most of the time this strain is picked up by others around.

Have you ever had a manager that was in constant turmoil? Liz's manager acted as if everything was a crisis and needed to be dealt with as soon as possible. This nervous energy trickled down to her group as they were pushed in many directions to put out "fires." However, the team didn't see them like that, just her manager. Liz's manager's stress was definitely felt by everyone on the team. It was tense and the days flew by because no one was present. Everyone on the team was focused on the perceived crisis. Eventually, Liz was moved to a different group with a different manager. Her new manager didn't live in crisis mode and Liz's days were much calmer. Her days slowed down and she was able to live more in the moment. She learned that every person is in charge of the way they handle situations. Crisis to one person may not be a crisis to another. It's based upon the perception of each individual. Being in a calmer environment led to happier and more present days for Liz.

Trust is an enduring and timeless quality. It is a vital part of all relationships. Have confidence in the Universe that it will take care of you. Allowing yourself to be in the present moment, instead of thinking of past hurts or future worries, gives you the peace to trust others. The present moment is the only real moment you have. Your memories can shape how you are today but the choice is yours to be and act differently. Start practicing trust and notice how your relationship with yourself, others, and the Universe take flight.

Trust plays a significant role in everyone's lives. Every day it takes practice to have confidence in the Universe, your best friend, or your husband. At times, when things aren't going the way you want them to go, it can be hard to trust the Universe. From your perception, you may see the world in a certain light. You may think that your life would be best with a certain job, at a certain weight, or in a particular house. Life as you know it looks different than what you'd imagined. As you begin to manifest your desires, the Universe will hear and deliver. This all takes trust. The magnificent Universe is always working with your best interest in mind.

Trust is built upon past occurrences. Look to see what the Universe has provided for you already. Do you have a house, children, and a loving husband? Do you have a good job, a car, and friends? Are your legs, arms, and fingers all in place? Most likely you have most of these things going for you in your life. Celebrate these things that you have, and have confidence in the Universe to continue to exemplify your life. This whole life is a process, there is no beginning or end. The main thing that matters is right now. These moments are shaping your life. Since there is no end, there is nowhere to go except for this present moment. Notice what you have in your life right now and trust in the Universe to provide.

When you see yourself beginning to worry, take a step back into the present. The moment you begin to worry is the moment when you have stepped into the future. The future hasn't happened yet. How many times have you worried about the future and when it finally came, it looked entirely different than you thought? Ninety-nine percent of the time the future does not look like we thought it would.

When we worry about the future, it only brings discomfort. Trust, with love, that everything happens for a reason. It may not make sense at the time but believe that it will turn out how it should.

Have you ever felt upset about an outcome that you thought would turn out differently? This will happen. Your mind is magnificent in that it has the ability to imagine potential situations. Usually, these scenarios don't look the way you thought they would, whether that is for better or for worse. When this happens, take a step back and be open to the current situation. Look at your thoughts on why you are satisfied or unsatisfied with the situation. What is your reason for being happy or upset? Do you have a belief about how something should or shouldn't be? Your beliefs are powerful and shape how you view the world. However, they can be examined and reassessed, if it serves you better. Is it possible to let go of a limiting belief and trust in the Universe? Knowing that it will deliver what is best for you at the right time.

For example, I believed in the fairytale romance from all of the movies I had seen. The man sweeps the woman off of her feet. He gives into her every desire and they live happily-ever-after. Nate definitely swept me off of my feet. However, as time went on, we came into a regular routine. At the time, I thought something was wrong with our relationship. I had the belief that the man should be "on" 100% of the time and vice versa. I examined my belief because I was distressed as I kept questioning his love for me. I realized that the fairytale romance isn't reality, as being 100% "on" is exhausting. Further, I realized that this reality was just as pleasant and beautiful. It had its own treasures. We felt comfortable. We trusted and respected each other. And most of all, we had a strong foundation in love. I was living the fairytale, it just looked different than what I thought it should look like. By examining my belief, I turned my thoughts and situation around. I stopped nagging Nate to be more romantic, the way I thought he should be. I saw how he was romantic, in his way, by having long conversations with me about his desires and goals, his interest in my life, and the way he was always looking for ways to improve our life together.

This is a lesson to learn about trusting the Universe. Every situation in life will turn out the best way possible for you. It is usually hindsight that gives us this insight. And that's okay because we are here to develop and live various circumstances. Each situation bears a gift, and it will expand you. The moments of awareness of these aids are the moments of expansion.

This life isn't what you have been told it is. It is not just about becoming a millionaire, being physically beautiful, or having fame. These things are what everyone has been taught to believe to have value. When you take a step back and think about this message, how does it make you feel? It makes me feel heavy. What a challenge to accomplish all of these things. And to top it off I am unworthy if I don't achieve these things! Instead, I would like to give you a different message. This message is from the Universe. It tells you that you have worth just by being born into this world. The magnificent human that you are is the gift to this world! When you expand into who you are, you will feel your worth. It's there already, you just need to believe it.

As you begin to open and feel your worthiness, trust in the Universe to deliver what you want. When I had several months seeking a job I learned and grew a lot in that experience. The journey looked quite different than I imagined. At times, that was tough on me. I would have high hopes for a potential job and then be let down when it didn't go the way I'd imagined. Each time I had to pick myself up and trust in the Universe. After some time, I got hired on at a cyber-security company. All the people that I had met were a blessing and an addition to my life.

Being in that space felt exactly where I needed to be. I don't believe that things just happen. I think I was placed in that particular place, at that time, for a reason. The message of that company was trust. I loved that message and what the company was accomplishing. I could see management's passion. They really wanted to do well.

Looking back, I can understand why each potential job wasn't the right fit for me. Besides what I could see, the Universe could see even more. The message of this particular company was something I completely agreed with. It was a beautiful thing to work for a business that had a message that I agreed with. I had asked the Universe to deliver a job that was fun, adventurous, had people that I could connect with, and where I could be a light in their lives. I desired a job that came effortlessly to me. Yes, the Universe heard me and brought that job to me.

During the interview process, I made it through all of the initial meetings and I was on my last one. I was going for a position that I didn't have any experience in (sales) but had other skills (technical and project management) to bring. Needless to say, the company wanted someone with more sales experience. As I heard the news, my heart was crushed. It took me some time to work through and process. My mind was telling me that I failed again, that I would never find a job, and that nobody wanted to hire me. Obviously, with those thoughts, I was not feeling my best. I knew that I had to apply the pure qualities to the situation.

Working through the pure qualities, I started with trust. Having confidence gave me the peace I was seeking. Something great was coming my way. I had asked for it. The Universe had never let me down before. Next, the pure quality of patience came to mind. Every situation requires patience. I didn't know what was ahead but I had to be patient. Additionally, I had to continue to love myself.

As I went through the qualities, I was centered again. A smile came across my face. You see, we are all human and all need to work through and remind ourselves of these pure qualities. They hold the answers for every situation.

During my phone conversation about the position that they did not think I was qualified for, they offered me another option. It would be an internal sales position. They would train me for six months about the art of selling and their business. The catch was that I would get paid half of what I was asking. This threw me for another loop. Here I had been in the engineering field for 10 years making twice as much money, so how could I take a step back? I really had to think this one through. It may have been a step back salary-wise but it was a step forward in a new area to learn and grow personally.

I decided to trust in the Universe and take the deal. Another pure quality mantra is to *try new things*. Who was I to say that this arrangement wouldn't lead to everything I had asked for and more? What I needed to remember was that I had asked and to trust that the Universe would deliver.

Life will always look different than you imagined. The beauty of it is the surprise and adventure of it all. The great news was that if I didn't like it, I had the choice to leave. Further, I had to trust that this job was exactly what I had asked for.

Taking a step back, I could see that the job had the potential for everything that I had asked for. The only part that was hard to swallow was the salary. However, I needed to look at the bigger picture. If I did well in sales, there was a commission. Besides that, there was value in many other aspects.

What my carnal mind defined as unworthy and unsatisfactory, the spiritual mind was jumping for joy. In my mind, I could only see the here and now, but my spiritual mind could see the big picture and knew that I was destined for exactly what I had asked for. Even though I don't work for them anymore, it was a valuable experience. I learned about trust, being open, and a new skill set, sales.

Where have you been disappointed to then realize that the situation was working out better than you imagined? When this happens, it is up to you to take notice and celebrate. By rejoicing and being grateful for what you do have, the Universe will be able to deliver more of that to you.

I am grateful for the job offer that I was given. What a gift that they saw my potential and wanted to take their time and money to train me. Also, I am grateful for that opportunity to have connected with new people. I was definitely grateful for the amount of money they did offer me. By being grateful for what I had, I was able to attract more of that into my life. My next job had the salary I wanted, more connections, and opportunities to learn. All of which were the things I loved about my previous job and that I had focused on daily. What could you be grateful for that if you were grateful would bring more of that in your life?

My situation could have been labeled as not ideal because I was making less money. However, the fact is, there is nothing bad or wrong in this world. It is only our perspective that creates our viewpoint. You can change your outlook, by believing that everything is working out for you. The key is to practice the pure quality of trust. For this to be easier, use love to guide you to that trust. You can do this by feeling the love that surrounds you and asking it to lead you. Have confidence that there is a larger force at play. And that is the perfect word, play. This is a playground, your playground.

That is why trust is so important because you don't know what wild success is around the corner. Once you are in a state of allowance for what your current situation is, then you can begin to manifest your next desire. The Universe is infinite. This is why you should trust it. This is why you must trust it. Be in allowance and focus on what is going right in your life. Be grateful, trust, and love.

Truth

Love is truthful; it shares its
true feelings, dreams, hopes,
and desires. It is authentic.

The truth will always feel lighter while a lie will feel heavy. Has anyone ever told you something that didn't feel right? Most likely there was a lie attached to what they were saying. The truth, with love, is a beautiful act. It is a pure quality that can be shared with strangers and loved ones. Communication, with loving truth, will bring connection to whoever uses it. The truth sheds light on any darkness. Use the truth to bring others and yourself life and love.

Thankfully, we all have an inner knowing or guidance system. This inner knowing guides us to see what is best for ourselves. There is also the outer chatter that is our programming from outside influences. This is usually from our parents, teachers, friends, political leaders, etc. They have their own outside influences that persuade what they say and think. We are all influenced by others. The good news is that we have our inner knowing that we can listen to instead. This voice is within you and will guide you whenever you pay attention to it.

First, know that you are loved by a powerful force outside of yourself. You are a gift to this world. Your life has a unique purpose. Particular people that you meet along the way are not by coincidence but for a reason. There are guides throughout your life that you will encounter. Lastly, you are unique and distinctive.

There is a reason why you came to this Earth at this time. As you begin to listen and take action, you will experience more light in your world. Trust your knowing because it's there to guide you and your purpose.

Your knowing can be as small as choosing which seat to sit on in an airplane. My husband and I usually sit next to each other when we fly. This last time we flew, I decided to pick two aisle seats next to each other. We both enjoy the aisle so instead of one person sitting in the middle, I changed it to both of us having an aisle seat. I ended up sitting next to a CEO of a high-tech data storage company. I just happened to be studying about high-tech data storage. This was an opportunity for me to learn exactly what I required. This little knowing of choosing to sit in this different seat was a gift. I didn't know it at the time; however, I chose it because it felt light and good for me. This is the inner knowing that guides everyone. This inner knowing is usually a light-hearted feeling. It's easy to follow. You just need to listen and take action.

When my husband and I had the big decision to move from Colorado to California for a work opportunity, it was tough. We both loved Colorado and didn't plan on ever moving from our home state. However, the opportunity felt right. We decided to make the move. Our inner knowing was guiding us that it was an opportunity for us and we should follow it.

Being in California for that year and a half, I can see the gift in it. The new friends and experiences were invaluable. Nate and I met people we wouldn't have met otherwise. This expanded our circle and reach. In the meantime, we were still able to keep our connections with our friends in Colorado. It wasn't easy moving to a new state. Every day I had to remind myself that there was a bigger purpose at play. In other words, growing and experiencing new things in life expands us. Spiritually, I developed a new sense of love and trust for myself and my husband because we had to lean on each other. In hindsight, I wouldn't take that time back. We were guided to that experience for many great reasons. Happily, we are back in Colorado enjoying a new home, our family, and friends.

The voice that guides you works on many levels and it is your reliable source. There may be times when you get an uneasy feeling. For example, someone is saying something to you that doesn't feel right. This person may be projecting their opinion onto you and it feels heavy. This is a moment to step back and realize that what they are saying is not truth for you. Your inner knowing is giving you the uneasy feeling. Take notice of this communication from your source. Know that you have what it takes to make the best decisions for yourself regardless of the opinion that this person is projecting. It's not always easy since there are many outside opinions. However, with practice, it will become easier for you to hear your inner voice.

It can be difficult to be truthful 100% of the time. Have you ever noticed how many times in a day you may be tempted to lie or do lie? It could be from telling your boss you were in the office at 8:00 AM instead of actually 8:15 AM or telling your dentist you floss every day. The truth is that a lie can seem like the easier option at times. However, telling the truth is important. When you share your truth with others, you may find more support than if you hadn't. For example, the dentist may have good advice on why it is important to floss every day and give you tips to stay motivated. You will also find that people can understand a situation better when the whole truth is given. Practicing the pure quality of truth on the smaller things will make it easier to use for the larger things in life.

Here is a possible everyday scenario: Cindy is a mom who wakes up to discover her children are in a cranky mood, not wanting to go to school. She has a busy day ahead of her including a meeting with the director of her company about recent sales. She is nervous, and her children's disdain of heading to school is bringing more stress into her day. Once she gets them to school and makes it to work, a co-worker asks her how she is. Cindy fakes a smile and says she is great. She doesn't want to have the persona that she isn't great all of the time. Also, she doesn't wish to get into it at work. As time moves closer for her meeting with the Director, she has several documents she still needs to prepare. Although stressed, she finishes on time for the meeting. At the meeting she is frank, to the point, and not very friendly. Her temperance has hit the ceiling. Although the meeting went well, it could have gone better.

What could she have done differently? How could openness have helped her in this situation?

Let's take another look at how the meeting could have gone for Cindy. Once her co-worker asked her how she was doing, Cindy could have been honest and said, "Not so great. My children were fighting against going to school today and I have several documents I need to finalize before my meeting with the Director."

Her colleague, if in the position to do so, can now empathize with Cindy and ask her how she can help. Knowing that Cindy needs help gives her colleague the opportunity to offer. By being truthful, another person is able to step-in and give Cindy the support she needs.

Her colleague happens to be able to help Cindy with one of the spreadsheets. She works concurrently with her, both completing the work before the meeting. When Cindy goes to her meeting, she is not stressed. She received the support of her colleague and was happy with the work they did. In the meeting, she was genuinely happy and impressed the Director. She made sure to give her co-worker credit for the document that she worked on. The Director was impressed with Cindy's final report and utilization of the team to get the job done.

Out of the two scenarios, sharing the truth that Cindy was stressed and had a deadline was the best thing for her. The Universe could then provide what she needed; it is always ready to provide you with what you need. It won't over-tax you with what you cannot do. As a human race, connected, it is important to work together. It is essential to keep in mind that everyone is going through something and could use a helping hand. Know and love that everyone has a story. There isn't a need to cover up or be fake about what you are going through.

Being truthful has many benefits. My good friend just got a promotion. It is for a more experienced job than she thinks she is qualified for; however, her boss thinks differently. All of this came about for her because she was honest. She told her boss that she wasn't happy where she was career-wise at her age nor with her salary. Truthfully, she was either going to find another job or she needed a promotion. I asked her how she had the guts to be so honest. Some people find it hard to be that truthful with their boss. She said that she had to be true to herself. She didn't like making that little sum of money for the amount of work she was doing. Further, there was no clear career path. She knew that she was in charge of her own career. The choice was ultimately hers. Her boss listened to her and liked her work ethic. He offered her the position even though he had been interviewing others. He told her that he thought she would be an excellent person for the job. She was promoted on the spot!

Because she was honest with herself, it was easy for her to be truthful with her boss. She took the time to listen to her inner knowing. Then, she took action. As she followed her truth, she was rewarded. These changes are natural in life if you allow yourself to be honest. It is okay to express how you feel and in this scenario it benefited my friend to be truthful with her boss.

In this situation, my friend could have predicted that her supervisor was going to deny her. This is a natural behavior to attempt to predict what will happen. These predictions can often be the worst-case scenario- it's human nature. Either way, I have never seen the most awful situation happen. Have you? When directed by truth, with love, then only good will result. What truth can you express that would bring more abundance into your life?

As you begin to practice truth with the smaller things in daily life, it will become easier. You will see the benefit of being truthful, such as Cindy did. You will notice that being honest isn't as bad or hard as it appears.

It's not always easy being truthful especially when you are afraid of negative judgment. My friend was diagnosed with a disease. She wanted me to keep it a secret because of the sad association it could bring. On the one hand, I completely understood, but on the other hand, I knew she could draw support from her closest friends and family if they knew. If she shared with them, she could draw strength from them and not be alone during a rocky period. (The truth is always your choice to give or not. It's a matter of knowing what's best for you.) For my friend, it was right for her not to share her diagnosis until she wanted. When she did, she got the support she needed. Sharing the information wasn't as bad as she thought. Further, she received much-needed support. However, sharing that information was ultimately up to her. She had to listen to her inner guidance for the right timing.

What has been the reaction of others when you have shared your authentic self? In my experience, people do not disown you. Instead, they want to help and give support. We all have ailments, issues, and problems. That is the human condition. By relying on your friends for support, you will get through anything. And of course, if the support of your friends disappears, then you may not want them in your life anyhow. Give them love and send them on their way.

We are taught from a young age to tell the truth. We get a little older, and we realize that the truth doesn't always get us what we want. In its place, we learn to tell white lies or small fibs. Most of the time little white lies won't kill a relationship and other times they do. However, it is truth in a relationship that will create a long lasting bond. It is important to share your real feelings, dreams, hopes, and desires. Being authentic is how to build healthy, love-filled, beautiful relationships.

In reality, the truth could be anything you want it to be. It is your perspective. When you explain a situation to someone, it is how you interpret it to be. Further, the situation that you have just explained will go through the filter of that person. Ultimately, the truth to you may be different than the truth to somebody else. Therefore, the question must be asked, "What is truth?" and "What is the truth to you?"

The complete truth, to your best ability, can help a confusing situation become clear. Someone may lie to protect someone else's feelings because there is uncertainty about how another will react. By doing this, though, this person is hiding her authentic self and deceiving the other person. For example, Tami, Jan, and Claire get together for dinner every month. Jan has a difficult personality. Every time they get together, Tami becomes quiet. Claire has never understood why but has never asked. The monthly dinners are a way for them to connect, but Tami is usually not herself. Tami doesn't like the way Jan talks poorly about other people. Tami hasn't shared this truth with Claire because she doesn't want to lose her friend, who seems to really enjoy Jan's company. If Tami decides to let Claire know why she becomes quiet around Jan, then this could explain any confusion that Claire has. Possibly, once Claire knows Tami's feelings, she can assure her that she values their friendship. She may even say that the next time Jan says something bad about someone else that she will speak up against it. At least, Claire now knows why Tami becomes so different around Jan. Claire knows it's not because of her. The truth can be a hard thing to deal with but with practice, it bears its fruit of aiding and benefiting your relationships.

Every relationship affects each person in it. It also affects other people that you may not even know that it does. As a child, you were affected by your parent's relationship with each other. There have been many studies showing the different effects of living in a home with two parents that are happy vs. being unhappy with each other. There is always some impact on the child. In this life, everyone is connected whether it is realized or not. The impact of your relationships reaches further than you know.

As humans, we observe each other, we judge and assess. Then, we put into practice what we have learned from our observations whether we decide to incorporate them into our lives or not. I was speaking with my good friend about some changes she was going through. She just got off of birth control after being on it for the last 14 years. Of course, her body was reacting to this new change with pimples, emotional swings, and lots of crying. At first, when the tears started to come, she had tried to stop them. She felt embarrassed to be crying in front of other people. Then, she questioned why she would stop the tears when it was a human emotion that she was feeling. After she had realized that, she didn't want to hold them back and she let her tears out.

She thought that if she could express her emotional truth in the present moment, then she would feel better, and it would allow others to open up about their emotions by following her example. Everyone needs guidance and direction in their lives. If you feel like crying or laughing, then why not let that out and be an example for others who are denying their truth?

Communicating our truth to others can be difficult. In *Nonviolent Communication: A Language of Life, 3rd Edition* by Marshall B. Rosenberg, Ph.D., he explains that we have automatic reactions. He says, "NVC [Non-violent communication] guides us in reframing how we express ourselves and hear others. Instead of habitual, automatic reactions, our words become conscious responses based firmly on awareness of what we are perceiving, feeling, and wanting. We are led to express ourselves with honesty and clarity, while simultaneously paying others a respectful and empathic attention" (Rosenberg, 2003).

He states that by knowing how to communicate, we can be open and honest about what we are feeling in a manner that allows the other person to be open to hearing what we are saying. In his book he discusses observing without evaluating, expressing feelings, and sustaining empathy. In regards to truth telling and how to communicate with your loved ones, I would recommend reading this book. For more information visit www.CNVC. org and www.NonviolentCommunication.com.

Emotions are necessary to express. The problem with how most people show them is that they put them on the other person. This released energy toward another person can be overwhelming. Every person is responsible for their own feelings. As you notice others projecting their feelings, watch your own feelings and see where you are sending them. Your feelings are yours. If you are on the receiving end and do not want the projected feelings, know that they are not yours. Return them to the sender. You don't have to receive or accept their feelings and emotions.

Knowing your feelings will allow you to take ownership of them. Your feelings are yours and no one else's. It is okay to express how you feel to someone else, but make sure that they know that these are your feelings.

Being human means that you will experience many emotions and feelings. At times, you may have even adopted someone else's feelings. Have you ever felt down because someone else was down? Adopting someone else's emotions is a common human trait. The good news is that you don't have to assume them. By having this new awareness, you can maintain a positive mood. You can empathize and practice the pure qualities with a friend in need, instead of being the one in need. Your friend's story is hers and not yours. Isn't that refreshing! Take note of emotions that others have and know that they are not yours.

Your inner guidance is always there to be truthful with you. It will always lead you to your truth. If listened to, your feelings about any situation will be revealed to you. Being honest with yourself and others is a benefit. Honesty is a pure, powerful quality that will enhance your life.

DISCIPLINE

*Love is disciplined; it
stays on the path of love,
relationship, and health.*

*D*iscipline is one of those words that receives unjustified condemnation. Any sentence with the word discipline sounds like it is going to be tough and painful. You are taught to be disciplined with your work, exercise, and the food you eat. No one ever says it takes discipline to throw a party or go on vacation. No, because those things are fun and easy, even though they do take a lot of work to plan. However, discipline is needed in all aspects of life. It is good to have, and it doesn't always have to be hard. The thing about discipline is that it takes work, but the reward outweighs the effort.

First, let us start off with the topic of discipline and your body. Being healthy for you and your body takes a good amount of control. Many books teach how to exercise and eat to maintain a healthy, long, disease-free life. Discipline with your body takes time and energy. It requires particular attention from personal care to movement. To move is to keep the blood flowing and muscles active. Having the discipline to exercise is being kind and loving to yourself.

How do you love yourself when you workout? Exercise can include any movement specifically for your body. There are many different types of movement such as stretching, walking, running, swimming, hiking, and biking. The particular exercise that you choose for your body is highly dependent on what works for you.

The road to health can be difficult! I know first-hand that there are many temptations. Then, to find myself exactly where I started a month earlier. I'm referring to yo-yo dieting. The cycle of being good and then falling off the wagon; indulging in everything that you missed while you were dieting.

The key is having balance as opposed to practicing extremes, which requires listening to your body. Your body is very communicative. When you stop and hear what your body has to say, you will hear its voice. Bodies start out quietly nudging to let you know that you are full or are eating something that isn't good for you. For example, some people get indigestion when they eat food that doesn't agree with their body. Then, it may move up to a skin rash or pimples. Some bodies even scream with joint pain or even cancer, saying, please stop eating food that is killing me. As this example may perhaps be dramatic, it does bear truth. Our bodies have a voice, and they will raise their voice when they need to. The good news is that we can begin listening to our bodies even if they are just whispering.

Ask your body, "What food would you like to eat?"

It may say, "Nothing, right now. I'm not hungry."

This response always surprises me if it has been longer than 4 hours since I last ate. I have a belief that I should be hungry if I haven't eaten in this amount of time; however, my body doesn't necessarily need food every four hours. Continue asking your body what it would like to eat. If you are at a restaurant, usually, your eyes will go directly to the item on the menu, if you ask this question. Your body already knows where the food item is on the menu. It is that smart, and it wants to guide you.

On a recent trip to Las Vegas, I discovered that my body didn't require three square meals. I was there for two days and ate a small breakfast and dinner. That was it. I was shocked that I was okay eating so little. I did not do this on purpose. When I asked my body if it was hungry, it wasn't. I didn't force the issue and demand that I eat. Instead, I honored my body and continued with my day. It was very easy.

At times, I find myself focused on what I'm going to eat for the day instead of what activities and adventure the day has in store for me. In Las Vegas, I was focused on the people and activities of the day. I was much more excited about this than the food I could eat. Usually, I would plan my day around what type of food I would like to experience. Instead, I focused on the current moment. I trusted that when my body became hungry; it would let me know. I didn't need to plan out all of my meals ahead of time. The food was in abundance in Las Vegas. When the time was right to eat I had the opportunity. I didn't have to worry.

The body is your teammate. It is on your side. Let it be the best teammate it can be. Think of your body as your best friend. Treat it as you would that person. Would you say nice or mean things to your best friend? Would you go out of your way to do something kind? When I think of my best friend, I consider the ways I can make her life more comfortable. Further, I try to make her laugh and feel good about herself. I compliment and never put down. I wouldn't tell my best friend that she was looking fat today. Neither would I tell her that she was awful at something (unless she truly was and she asked for constructive feedback, which I would give rooted in love). Instead, I would praise her on how well she looked in her shirt or how great her hair was. How can you start treating your body as you would your best friend?

My journey with food has been eye-opening. I have had eczema my whole life. My legs used to have severe scrapes on them because I would be very itchy and scratch them. In fourth grade, my girlfriend's mother called the child abuse center. She thought that abuse was occurring in my home. I explained that I had eczema and was very itchy all of the time. They understood and didn't ask any more questions. Eczema was a common ailment of living in the very dry climate of Colorado. I struggled with this itchiness for most of my life.

As I began asking questions of what food my body wanted, answers came. At first, I experimented with wheat-free and dairy-free products. Removing these types of foods helped a little, although I would still be itchy after I had a wheat-free and dairy-free meal, such as sushi. I was confused because I would feel better after eating most wheat-free and dairy-free foods. I concluded that I did not have an allergy to these ingredients but still refrained from them as much as I could. I wasn't strict about it and still had symptoms. Then, the gluten-free awareness came out onto the scene. I decided to give this a try, and my itchiness went away. It was a miracle or, at least, a life-changing revelation. I got tested for a gluten intolerance, and it came out positive. I now knew why I was still itchy after eating sushi because soy sauce had gluten in it.

I've also noticed that soy products will cause me to break out with acne. Therefore, I avoid soy products such as soy milk and tofu. Your body is unique and has specific requirements. It houses your spirit and gives you the ability to experience life, so enjoy it pain-free! Figuring out what is safe and healthy for your body is a process, but one that is well worth it.

Having the knowledge of what is good for your body is a great first step. However, it takes discipline to follow through. It takes will-power not to have a cookie with gluten in it. I have to refrain from quite a few foods. The good news is that there are substitutions. And the better news is that because I love myself so much I can be disciplined. This is the gift of this pure quality.

Life requires discipline, including the food we eat. Determination can hold you for so long, but that takes a lot of effort. Instead, practice discipline with love for yourself. It will be much easier to refrain from the food that doesn't agree with you.

Your body is your housing while on this earth. It gets you from place to place so you can interact with other people, travel the world, and enjoy this planet. It should be treated with care. Over indulging and eating poor food does not help your body to have a healthy and happy life. A positive difference in your life can be experienced by avoiding the types of foods that make you lethargic and overweight. Being too heavy could make it challenging to enjoy all the possibilities of life.

Discipline is a work in action. It is a process that improves over time. A 16-year-old, first-time driver, won't be as good as a 35-year-old driver of 19 years. It takes practice to develop. Further, it takes self-love to stay on the path of discipline and self-care for your body. Love is the lesson in this journey. The key to weight loss is love. The actionable word, love, and not just the emotion.

First, to love oneself on the path to weight loss is to forgive yourself for any past indulgences and any future ones. Next, journal about how you envision your life. Do you see yourself traveling, hiking a beautiful mountain, or playing ball with your children? Next, do whatever feels right for you. Exercise in whatever movement is best for you at the time. Your body is meant to move, whether that is walking, running, weight-lifting, or dancing. On different days, I feel like doing different types of movement. Some days I enjoy Zumba while others yoga. I have even found myself playing golf, which was an unexpected sport for me to play. I listen to my body and hear what is best for it at the time. Thankfully, there are a wide variety of activities to choose from. What do you enjoy the most? When temptation arises, remember your vision and to practice self-love.

When I went to dinner with my friends last week I consciously practiced discipline. Beforehand I knew that

I would need to implement it, with love. Many times in the past I have been tempted by indulging in too many drinks and food that did not sit well with me. Since I had been practicing discipline in my daily life, it was easier not to give into temptation.

For example, one of my friends ordered several different appetizers at the restaurant including sweet bacon, fried zucchini, and veggies with hummus. Since I had been practicing discipline during the week, on less tempting items, I was able to think through my eating decisions. I chose to eat the veggies with hummus and stay away from the sweet bacon and fried zucchini. Remembering that in the past, I have felt too full, bloated, and unenergetic after having that food. This decision worked for me as I knew those types of foods usually did not agree with me. It wasn't a hard decision as I could hear my body and, with love, chose the right food for me at that time.

Usually, on the weekends, I am influenced by my friend's food choices. Being influenced by other's choices is a natural phenomenon. There have been studies showing that the first person to order has an impact on the rest of the table. For example, if the first person orders a salad, the other people will rethink their decision for a healthier option if they were going to choose something not as healthy. The same if someone orders dessert, others will follow.

As in my recent example, it is important to remember that my friends have the choice with their needs and discipline. I have the choice to order food that aligns with my needs and discipline. Most likely, they are different. However, I can still be influenced by their decisions and vice versa. As the pure quality of discipline grows, it is easier to hear your inner voice and choose what is right for you.

When you find yourself in a situation where you are tempted to eat or drink something you intuitively know your body doesn't want, just be aware. Having that awareness is the first step to making a different choice. Ultimately, empowering you to create a different path that is healing and healthy for you and your body. Lastly, practicing discipline in all of the small areas of your life will give you strength for the bigger areas in your life. It will become easier for you with every situation.

For instance, you find yourself out with friends and someone orders french fries for the table. Knowing that this particular type of food gives you indigestion and guilt after eating them, you decide to refrain. It comes with no trouble to you because you are in communication with your body. Afterward, you are rewarded with no indigestion pain or guilt.

By practicing the pure quality of discipline, you were aware that eating that type of food would hurt your body. You knew that when tempted, you had a choice. You recognized what is right for you and what is not. If something is going to give you guilt after eating it, then why not avoid it?

As you begin to practice the pure quality of discipline, you will find that it is easier to implement it into your life. Remember the gift that the Universe is teaching is to learn about love, and these qualities define it. When practiced, love and joy are felt to the core. It is the practice of these qualities that connects you with others and the Universe. In turn, you will feel the love and peace that you are seeking in everything that you do. Practice in the times when it is easy, and it will spill over into the times that are difficult. In that, you will find that it isn't so difficult anymore.

The next time temptation comes remember that you love yourself and want the best for yourself. Usually, you know the difference between what you should and should not be doing, it's a gut feeling or thought in the back of your head. You intuitively know what decisions are good or bad for you. It is a matter of practicing and growing this quality within you to recognize it faster and, therefore, respond quicker resulting in fewer regrets. Luckily, you have been given many avenues to practice discipline in the way you think, act, and talk.

Every day takes practice. Besides the positive aspects of having discipline with your body and food, it can be a benefit in every aspect of your life. It plays a role in all areas of your behavior. For example, keeping your promises. Have you ever broken a commitment? To not break one, takes discipline. It may not always be easy because you may feel tired or unmotivated. However, following through with your word will have a positive outcome in your life.

Going to work every day takes discipline. This is a commitment that you have made with your employer. There are days that you don't want to go to work. When you show up for these days still, you are practicing the pure quality of discipline. As this practice matures and grows inside of you, you will reap the rewards. Your boss and co-workers will notice. They will learn that you are responsible and reliable. When they need someone like you in their court, they will call upon you. It is that easy! Abundance will come knocking on your door. And of course, practice with love. It is the love portion that gives the qualities their power. The qualities are expressions of love, and they require it for the full effect.

Being in the corporate world, I am disciplined by showing up for work and giving my best. I do this because I know that it is the right thing to do, for me. It feels good inside when I show up. Others know that they can count on me. They can trust me. Besides feeling good, I also have a growing skill set and a list of accomplishments on my resume.

The other day I specifically focused on the pure quality of discipline. Here is how it turned out:

The night before I wrote out what I would like to accomplish the following day. My list included eating well, bringing my best to work, staying focused, and staying true to myself. I checked in with my body to see how I could be of service to it. Since I enjoy moving my body, I decided to go for a run first thing in the morning. It took discipline to get out of bed an hour earlier. When the alarm went off, I wanted to hit snooze, but I knew that the decision I made the night before to go running would be a benefit to my body and spirit. By doing this, I setup the rest of my day to feel energized and connected to nature. During my run, I began to wake up and feel invigorated. I got to admire all of the beautiful yards with colorful flowers, bushes, and trees. Plus, there were plenty of birds to observe as they flew around, busy with their morning routine.

Being focused on discipline brought my attention to my list throughout the day. Lately at work, my back has been hurting from slouching while working at the computer. Therefore, I noted to sit with good posture. Another way I practiced was in my meetings. My mind has the tendency to wander so I practiced staying present and actively listening.

To stay true to myself, at work, I removed negative thinking about myself. At times, I get nervous when my manager asks me to do something, and I'm not exactly sure how to do it. I become afraid to ask questions because I believe I should already know. On this day, I was requested to create business slides. However, the directions weren't clear. Due to lack of time, I wasn't able to ask questions. My head instantly clouded, and I was confused about what to do. To honor my self-love practice, I reminded myself that it was okay if I didn't know what to do completely and to do my best. Therefore, I came up with a list of questions to ask later when my manager was available. As soon as I approached him, he was very open to answering my questions.

Practicing discipline improved all aspects of my day. From the start, I honored my body with a run outside. Further, I was present at my meetings and brought my best self to conscious focus. Lastly, I stayed true to myself and stopped negative thinking. How could the practice of discipline change your day?

In this life, there are accomplishments and achievements. People will judge and measure upon these. It is not about being the best or having the most. It is about what you have done that is just right for you and your life. At times, you may have the thought that you need to rise above the rest. And that it is important to be better than everyone else. What if I told you that you can still have all that you desire without this heavy burden?

Imagine that you are standing alone on a big boulder. You are looking out over the world. You can see all the buildings, people, and cars below. You take a deep breath in and exhale. You know that what you have to offer is important and valuable. You came to this Earth, at this time, for a reason. You smile quietly to yourself. You know what you must do. It doesn't entail being better than anyone else. It doesn't include fighting to the top, having an expensive car, or a large house. Your purpose is bigger than those physical things. It's expansive, inclusive, and filled with love. What you have to offer the world doesn't include comparing yourself to others. It is being exactly who you are.

For many years, I believed that I needed to be a successful corporate business woman to be valuable. I thought this was the only way. I got this idea from movies I had watched. Now I see that my value does not come from this definition. Instead, it comes from having a close and loving family, a great network of friends, hobbies that bring me enjoyment, and a job that I like. And ultimately, I am valuable by just being me with my family, friends, and at work. Honoring, who I am, is the "value" I was seeking.

I don't value rising to the top of the corporate ladder anymore. I appreciate feeling good about me and enjoying life to its fullest. To know this gives me happiness in every moment. Are there beliefs that you have that aren't creating the most joyful life for you? Consider if you focused on what brings you joy. Would your life look differently?

As you practice these qualities, with love, your path will illuminate. The path that you are seeking is waiting for you. Consider following the lightness and it will take you exactly where you want to go. The way of discipline is gratifying.

Following your path takes devoted attention. When you wake up in the morning, stir up the feelings of excitement for you. It can be a descriptive word such as *adventure*, *fun*, or *peace*. Then, think of a time when you have felt this. As you stir up this emotion inside of you, it will build a momentum for the day. Implementing this activity takes practice but it comes with significant rewards.

Every morning I think of a descriptive word such as happiness. I begin to smile and think of being happy. As I move throughout my day, I am aware of all the moments that I am happy. My cheerfulness only grows as the day continues. At the end of the day, I notice that I have had a joyful day, and it all started with the thought of happiness that morning. What descriptive word would make you feel good that you can think about as soon as you wake up?

Connecting with what you are passionate about is another facet to apply the act of discipline. What excites you? I understand that at first this can seem hard to figure out. To begin to discover your passions, have awareness during the day of what makes you smile. It may be your children, pets, or your husband. It could be nature. Take a moment to be grateful for what makes you smile. By focusing your attention on that, it will build momentum for more similar things that make you happy. Eventually, you will be able to pinpoint several things that excite you. It could be spending time with others, taking care of animals, or cooking. After you have figured out what brings you bliss, do more of it. Stir up that exciting feeling that brings you joy. Take the time to notice, be aware, and take action.

For me, I love building relationships and connecting people. I get very excited thinking about this. I love to throw parties and events that help others connect. During an event, I like to find out about people's interests and connect them with others that will be a benefit to them. I get joy out of this connection, and I continue to throw parties so I can feel this satisfaction.

Also, I love seeing what excites my mom and sister and when they act on their desires. They have a strong urge for being near the ocean. They love spending their time there. When they are there, they feel calm and peaceful. They know that to feel inner peace they need to visit the ocean continually. Even as you are reading this, I am sure they are either by the ocean or planning a trip to be near it. This is what makes them feel good and they continue to bring more of this into their lives, just for the sheer enjoyment of it.

Lastly, my husband enjoys learning about gems and minerals. He has a deep passion for this beautiful part of nature. When he has free time, he immerses himself in this subject. Geology excites him, and he makes sure to spend time on this passion of his. Besides having a large collection of gems and minerals, he visits gem and mineral shows. Yes, they exist! He will spend days looking at the various vendor's collections of gems and minerals. He always ends up with a few specimens to bring home just for the pleasure it brings to his spirit. What is your passion that puts a smile on your face?

The act of discipline is a pure quality because it is a component of love. As every pure quality brings you closer to love, discipline is a method on that path. You have already incorporated this into your life from taking care of your health to going to work. You have done this because you have seen the benefits. Either you felt good physically or mentally by practicing discipline. The joy of discipline is one of the keys to living the life you came here to live. It is a proven process for abundance in your life. By being disciplined and discovering your passion, you will experience more of that internal joyful feeling that you enjoy.

Understanding

Love is understanding; it continually
asks questions to know one
another through all of life.

If you understand one thing, understand that life isn't about your accomplishments; it is about your relationships with those around you. Each of us has our perception and beliefs about the world. In this vision that you have created and that others have created, you will fit well or not together. The connections you make are made for a reason- that you experience the lessons and relationships that are right for you. You have a journey to fulfill, and the right people and experiences will come your way.

When you don't get what you want, there is a reason. Understand that there is a unique purpose for your life. For example, if you don't get the job you wanted, trust that there is a reason. Consider that the people and circumstances wouldn't have been the right fit for what you needed to experience. Second, know that there is a better fit coming your way. Understand and trust in this knowing.

At some point, you will be able to see the reason for the connections that you have made. The big picture of how and why your life played out the way it did will come into focus. Instead of stressing over not getting what you want in the way that you pictured it, understand that there is a purpose for the way it has played out. When a door closes, allow it. When another opens, follow it through. There is a reason for all of it. Know that each area in your life and your connections with people are for a reason. This is your path. It's easy to follow if you accept and allow it to unfold organically.

Relationship building is a vital part of all of our lives. Getting to know each other through questions connects and solidifies who we are with others. Questions are powerful and should be used as much as possible to give more understanding. Asking questions and receiving answers are a way to connect you with everyone and everything. It is through this process that you open yourself to possibilities because you are open to the answers; you are living in the question which means infinite possibility exists for you.

As you go through this life, it is essential to ask why and how things are the way they are. For many of our questions, we have solidified answers such as "Do you have any pets?" Answer: "Yes, I have two dogs." However, there are some answers that many believe they already have, and so they stop questioning. Do you question how much fun you will have at work? Or have you already concluded this question with a solid answer? Everyone has conclusions in place; questions that have certain answers without the urge to question them. Usually, these are referred to as our beliefs. Firmly, we hold our beliefs as truth and rarely question them.

Back at the beginning of your life, when you were a child, every day was an adventure, and you questioned what fun surprises would come your way. You didn't know what adventures you would have that day, but you intuitively asked and expected they would come. You were open to the answers.

Questioning everything you do is living your life in the question; never knowing what will happen next but expecting great things to be coming your way. By living this way, there is excitement and trust that the Universe is working on your behalf.

Do you remember how much fun you had as a child? Do you think it had anything to do with you living in the moment of what fun or adventure you would have that day? As an adult, you have answered this question already. You already have judgments and conclusions in place. For example, you have already defined the amount of fun you will have at work. Most likely you have concluded that you will wait to have a good time until the weekend. When you have made this conclusion about the amount of fun you will have at work, then that is what you will have. You create your reality. Instead, ask the Universe about what fun and adventure you will have at work that day. Do you think that you will have a different experience at work? Give it a try.

In your lifetime, many conclusions will be formed. Each one will dictate your behavior. When a conclusion exists, it will guide you in all of your decisions. An easy example to understand is with food. Let's say Kayla has the conclusion that chocolate is not good for her. With this conclusion, she may avoid chocolate at all costs. This decision may be a deprivation for her body of the nutrients in chocolate. A better way is for her to remove this conclusion and become centered with her body; asking it what it requires and listening for the answer that is right for her.

My sister taught me always to ask my body what it would like: "Body, would you like to eat chocolate? How much chocolate would you like to have?"

Then, listen to your body and have as much as it says you can have. As I mentioned earlier, you can learn more about her methodology in her book, *Your Body Relationship,* by Christina Duskis, which I recommend for more peace in your relationship with your body. Asking your body if it desires a particular food and how much is living in the question.

If you conclude that chocolate is not good for you then eat chocolate anyhow; it will most likely make you feel unpleasant, either mentally or physically. If you ask, then you are living in the question of now as opposed to a conclusion you have made based on a past belief. Questioning is a powerful tool and helps you to understand any situation. When you ask questions, awareness and understanding come, and that is bringing love into your life instead of confusion and conclusion.

Understanding another person's situation helps to relate. The pure quality, understanding is the foundation of any relationship, which is what is so great about this quality. You have the ability to put yourself in other people's shoes so you can have compassion for them. When you understand, you can be more tolerant because you would want others to be tolerant of you if you were in the same position. Is there a situation in your life where you could be more understanding if you put yourself in another's shoes? Have you been through something that helped you understand someone else's behavior better?

My friend Carrie has a strong personality. She comes across as a know-it-all. When I first met her, this caught me off-guard. Her opinion was something that she did not hold back. If she felt strong about something, she made sure that you knew it. Her attitude was opposite of mine. At first, I had a hard time liking her. Of course, this was hard for me as I like to get along with everyone right away. I struggled with this new relationship. I practiced the pure quality of understanding. I knew that there must be more for me to learn. After all, she had come into my life for a reason. I continued to practice patience and understanding, with love, for her. Instead of focusing on what I didn't like, I focused on finding things I did like. I got to know her. With each encounter, I learned a different side of Carrie and why she was the way she was. Her upbringing and family played a significant role in who she was. She was taught to be confident in what she knows. Further, when she does know something, to share that information, as a way of helping others. I came to a new appreciation and understanding of her.

By practicing understanding, I gained a new friend. She has a different perspective on life than I am used to. I learned to be open to her personality. It was easy for me to judge her in the beginning because I didn't know her. I had my conclusions about how a person should behave, and she didn't fall into that. However, instead of resisting her, I embraced that I needed to understand her better. Who have you been uncomfortable around because you didn't understand them? Every person comes into your life for a reason. It may not be clear at the time but by practicing the pure qualities, there are answers for everything. Let the way of love guide you.

Once you begin to understand, then you can change. Your power is in the ability to transform. Knowing the inner workings of a system gives way to understanding the system. For example, many of us are involved in some system. Some of these systems that you may be familiar with include dieting and exercise programs and religious organizations. All of them have a method to guide your actions and to help you become the person that you desire to be. They all teach you a way to behave. Many people want this type of hold in their life to feel in control of themselves. Some do not feel they can live life without a rule system to follow. But, what if there was another way? What if by letting go of control, you could be in control? Is it possible that by following one of these programs to feel in control is actually making you feel out of control?

When you follow a program, it is inevitable that you will slip up; you will fail at some point. When this occurs, you will feel sorry and believe that you are a failure. Programs enlist rules into your life. At any time, these rules can be added or removed. Any rules that you put on yourself can be simply eliminated by yourself as this is a matter of perception and your belief system. When you have a rule in place that you cannot eat bread, and then you do eat bread, you have just judged yourself as bad. However if the rule did not exist and you ate bread, there would be no judgment. You are your beliefs, and you have the power to change those beliefs at any time. You can tune into your inner guidance system and hear its wisdom at any time.

It is desirable to many to have a system or program in place to feel in control. However, in reality, these systems actually can make one feel out of control. In the church that I grew up in, there were many rules. We were not allowed to wear makeup, skirts needed to be below the knee, and we couldn't do any work on the Sabbath. We followed these rules because we believed that this was the right way of life. We felt righteous and good about ourselves. When I got older, I decided that I liked wearing makeup. I thought it made me look more put together and professional. However, I felt very guilty for doing so. I had to struggle with my belief that it was wrong. I decided to let go. In this way, I was letting go of control in my life. Guess what happened? I felt good about myself and the new makeup that I was wearing. I was "out of control" but felt in control of how I looked and felt good about it. How can this relate to your life? Is there a belief system that you have to keep you in control of your life but, in reality, is making you feel out of control?

I have tried many diet plans. I have felt the craziness of being in and out of control with them. At first, I would feel in control following the plan. However, I would always fall off the wagon. It was miserable. Regretful thoughts would plague me, such as, "I shouldn't have eaten those chips last night," or, "I shouldn't have had a glass of wine with dinner," or, "I will not eat anything tomorrow to make up for what I ate last night."

The negative chatter was endless. The only reason these thoughts emerged is because I believed that chips and wine were bad and that minimizing my food intake would be the answer. By being in control, I was out of control. To be in control, I propose a new plan: let go, trust, and live. Trust your inner guidance system. Rely on it for the answers to your questions. You can do it. It will be scary and exhilarating.

Next time you hear negative chatter turn it around into something positive. Go with the flow and accept that you did the action and that it is okay. It is what it is. The moment you decide to let go is the moment that blessings will spill forth into your life. The Universe is here to guide and protect you. Why do you think you can do what the Universe is here to do for you better? Listen to your inner knowing and ask for understanding of all things. The clarity that you seek will be known to you.

The process of understanding can be long and tedious, yet it is vital to living. Everyday living requires it, from taking care of you to being functional in society. It is the process of gaining knowledge and answering your questions of why. Once you understand a certain topic, issue, or circumstance, you will stop asking why. It's funny because children around the age of three go through their most prominent "why" stage, but the fact of the matter is that this phase continues for life. You will find yourself asking the following questions through life: Why does that behave the way it does? Why did that happen? Why is this the way it is? Why? Why? Why? And of course, the proper answer to any question that begins with a why is with a "Because..." This response is the beginning of trying to help one to gain understanding to their question. Life is about learning, understanding, and growing. Therefore, this essential pure quality is vital to your very well-being.

This pure quality is life giving. By practicing this, you will see your life flourish as well as experience more love in your life. This is to be practiced daily to have the most enrichment in your life.

Another aspect of understanding is to realize the gift you are. You were born with many talents to be discovered. All of these abilities are for you to receive and to be a gift to others. By understanding how wonderful you are then, you can live your best life. It may take a lot or a little practice to realize the gift you are, however, it is well worth it. To start, notice when others compliment you. This will be a clue. Do you have a gift for making others feel noticed and special? Recognize that you have many gifts. Acknowledging your talents and abilities help you to understand how special you are. Once you understand this, then you can use this information to feel good about you. Ultimately, the goal is to resonate with self-love, which is impenetrable.

One morning I was beaming with energy after listening to an uplifting self-help audio book. I was feeling inspired and full of love. On the train to San Francisco, there was an overbearing, agitated gentleman. The train was crowded, and people were standing. He was vocal in letting others know not to stand in front of him. On his exit, he bumped into a lady. He didn't apologize. His action startled her, and she seemed like she was about to get upset. I asked her if she was okay and that he was obviously having a bad day. I wanted to be encouraging and to let her know she had someone on her side so I said, "We won't let him affect us."

She said, "Thank you," and smiled.

I believe that my gift for her was my positive energy. Instead of the momentum building from that point forward and throughout her day, we were able to counteract it with love. Truly, I believe we all have this gift, and this was mine to share at that moment.

Speaking of momentum, it is an exceptional force in our lives. As I have mentioned before, starting your day off with a positive thought is very beneficial. This could be a statement such as, "Today I am grateful to be alive! I am beautiful, healthy, and happy! What would it take to have a fantastic day?"

Just these few thoughts will set the momentum for the day. A positive statement such as these sets into motion a light and happy feeling, which focuses your attention on more light and happy thoughts. It is just like a snowball racing down a hill; it gets bigger and moves faster as it gets closer to the bottom. It is building momentum. I could give you an example of a negative statement, but I'd rather not focus on that. Being grateful for what you have at the moment is an excellent way to start each day. Understanding this concept will bring more love and peace into your life.

Not only do I see that my energy has a positive impact on many people, I know it. Not everyone has the energy or positive attitude that I have. I say this with confidence because I want to illustrate that you should be confident in your abilities too!

When you give a gift to a friend, do you want them to love it and use it? Or do you want them to discard it and say that they didn't like it? I will assume that you would want them to love it or at least like it. The same is for the gifts that you have. Appreciate and enjoy them. You have many talents. Get to know and understand your unique skills and magnify and share them for all to enjoy, including yourself. What capabilities do you have that if you realize and understand them, would open more doors than you ever imagined?

Due to the high amount of energy and positive attitude that I have, I smile a lot. I have many people tell me that they noticed me because I was the "smiley one." How many people have been great connections just because I smiled? Many! Moreover, each of these people have been a benefit in my life. It is fun to converse and share life with others. Understanding what your capabilities are will make every day better because then you can focus on those unique talents. Isn't it fun to understand who you are and the fun abilities you possess?

You may be thinking that having a positive attitude or lots of energy isn't a talent. Instead, you may believe that being outstanding in math or science is. Of course, I would say that you are right that being good at math and science is a gift. So many critical technologies and advancements exist due to people with abilities in these areas. On the other hand, many enjoyments have been created by people with a positive attitude and an abundance of energy. These are all talents! Only a judgment or conclusion that something is not a talent is a limiting belief.

Every person has many capabilities even if society has labeled one differently. Further, everyone is a gift to this world. Even the homeless person on the corner begging for money is a gift. Either someone can feel good about giving him money or someone can be reminded to be grateful for what he has. Everything has a gift in it if you are willing to perceive it. Seeing is understanding.

Realizing that you are special and have many talents is crucial to knowing who you are. Whenever you doubt this, fill up with love. Use the pure quality of understanding to know how your talents and abilities are a positive in your life and other's lives. Write them down on a sticky note and place it on your bathroom mirror. Every morning, read the talents that you embody out loud. You will begin to understand and start your day off with momentum in a positive and loving direction.

LOVE

*Love is the key to all of
the pure qualities.*

$\mathcal{B}$e immersed in the love that is surrounding you. Touch, sight, sound, and the feeling of love emanates all around you. Your awareness can be heightened to this if you are open to hearing it, feeling it, and experiencing it right now. Being encompassed in love is bliss and yours to experience if you are open to it. With love, all things are possible. Without it, only worry and stress exist.

Love changes everything. The way we view the world, people, places...it all changes. With love, a whole new world exists and the eyes are open to a new existence. Why is it this way? Because with love, only pureness can thrive. It is the collaboration of human life and love that makes everything beautiful and synergistic.

As you place your eyes on another, and you don't see their beauty, it is because there is not love to bring your awareness into full force. You may be an English woman and see an Indian woman. You notice the difference in your color and your culture. You have separated yourself, and you don't see any resemblance. As time goes by, you have experiences with this Indian woman; you go to the same gym and shop at the same grocery store. Slowly you begin to notice each other. Eventually, at one point, you are next to each other in an exercise class. You begin to talk and realize that you have a lot in common. As well as many differences, but these differences fascinate you. She has children, as you do. She loves to experience the local museums, and she even has a similar love of history and art. What once was someone you separated yourself from is now a friend. You begin building a fruitful relationship. The bond between you is recognizable.

Now imagine this type of relationship from the beginning, without the time and space in between. Before knowing your friend you have love in your heart for her instantly. You have respect and adoration for this person from the love in your spirit toward another fellow spirit. Only with love in your heart can this happen. Love for the human race. Love for your sister or brother. Having this type of love will change your world, love for everyone and everything. What would your life be like then? Would it be more beautiful than it is now? Love changes everything.

One of the things that I like to do is to imagine everyone as they were as a child. You can see the childlike fun in everyone's eyes and the curl of their lips as they smile. I haven't met one person that doesn't have this innocence inside of them from C-level executives to a mother, friend, or stranger. They all have this same likeness. They all want to feel and be loved. It is in their core nature. Speak to them as they are, beautiful humans desiring to be valued. You can give them this love, easily. It is within you. Trust me, by giving your loving kindness you will receive it in abundance. By giving, you receive, and it is in a way that you never imagined.

Love is magical and beautiful. It is yours to provide and have. Feel deep down in your heart the love that you have. To stir up your love, imagine spending time with a close friend or family member. As you talk freely, listen deeply, and have good intentions in your heart, see yourself laughing and notice the happiness on your face and in your soul. You are joyful and are embracing the love within you. Take this love feeling and apply it to other situations. Get to know this feeling of love and be able to access it purposefully.

Understand that love is within you and that you can share it. As a human, you have the key to an incredible life of connection and inner peace. Achieving this state of being is as easy as sharing the love within you, with others. The first step is to care genuinely about others. See the good in them. See them as you are, just another part of who you are. Honestly understand them. By doing this, you will be giving others a gift; feeling and seeing who they truly are. Everyone wants and needs to feel worthy. By you giving them this gift they will open their heart because it is the genuine true calling to feel this within the human soul. Remember that you are special. You are worthy. You have the love within you to complete the hole in others and vice versa you will feel whole.

Imagine a life without your love. Then, further, imagine life without other's love. The world would not exist. It's all interconnected. As you love and others love, the world continues its mission to bring everyone together through the bond of love.

Love is needed to survive even from when you were an infant. Your parents or a care giver gave you this unconditional love. Naturally, you were drawn to them to feel loved and to be nourished.

Everyone is seeking love, value, and worth. Not only is this powerful force of love within your ability it is who you are. You are as close as you want to be to it. It is yours for the taking and yours for the giving. Life is love, and love is life.

The power of these pure qualities is beautiful. Pure qualities such as these bring inner peace, friendship, and kindness to your spirit and soul. Practice and learn about these special attributes of the Universe. This combination of qualities will bring transformation into your life and relationships.

Life is full of energy. When you spend your energy on encouraging others, you are bringing joy to their life. Everyone needs encouragement from each other. When you do this, you are lifting others to higher heights. Then, as a collective whole, the human race can flourish with the support of each other. Building any relationship is developing the support system that is needed to live life joyfully. The way to do this is to spend time with others such as eating together, playing a sport, taking a walk or calling someone and sharing your life experiences.

The more you experience and open yourself up to in life, the more you will learn about yourself and others. Say

"Yes!" more often to trying new things. You may find more joy when you say yes to life and more joy when you do these new things with people. As Ralph Waldo Emerson said, "It is not length of life, but depth of life."

There are many aspects of the pure qualities. For example, being quiet births joy. As you learn to be quiet and listen to others and yourself, you will find a joy bubble up inside of you. First of all, you will be learning about others. Secondly, you will be learning about yourself. This will bring joy to your life as you learn about your passions and incorporate them into your life.

Further, you can give a helping hand to a friend because you have listened to what their passions are. Once you have figured out your joy, such as spending time with family or friends, writing, golfing or singing then you can share your joy with others. Let them in on your joy and spread it to them. Also, share in their joy, this is a two-way street. Be joyful, have fun, think positive, and be optimistic. Share the joy amongst each other.

Love is an action and to love, one needs to be able to show it. From the beginning of this book, you have been learning (and hopefully practicing) how to show love with your actions. The Love Formula gives ways to practice love by expressing love to others and yourself. Love is gentle, quiet, and listens to others. Love understands other people's situations and circumstances; it forgives quickly. Being patient a little longer than normal is another act of love. It asks what you can do for others; do all of these things with love. Love benefits and strengthens relationships. In "The Love Chapter" in the Bible it states, "If I give all I possess to the poor and give over my body to hardship that I may boast, but do not have love, I gain nothing" (Holy Bible N. I., Bible Gateway, 1 Cor. 13:3). In other words, without love, everything else is profitless.

In any and all circumstances, you are given the ability to love. Every opportunity could be rooted in love if you choose. The game of this world is to give and receive love at all times. Judgment hinders love. This blocking of love only brings separation. Notice the difference in yourself and others but without judgment. There are many different types, sizes, and shapes of people. All built with a special mission and a unique state of mind. These are your fellow spirits, in this lifetime, on this Earth. It can be confusing to see all the different angles of the human race. Rest assured that all you need is love, for it all. For any questions, concerns, possibilities, and adventures; all that is required is your love. Your particular love to seal the deal. As your presence transcends the first line of defense, trust in it. Your message is within you to share. This message, when rooted in love, will be the answer, your key to unlocking what you desire.

At a conference, I noticed all the people rushing past me. I too rushed past them. They all had agendas, including me. What I noticed is that these people were going nowhere fast. Life is as easy as pulling the curtain open when you choose and so this is what I did. I stopped what I was doing and noticed what was going on around me. Trying to "accomplish something" was leading to nowhere. The more rushing and trying I did at the conference, the more lost and confused I felt. Where was everyone going? What was everyone doing here?

I spoke with a salesman for a software feature for a well-known software company. He gave me his sales pitch, and I listened, noticing that he was beginning to sweat. Why was he sweating? Did I make him nervous? At that moment, I listened more intently to what he had to say to give him some comfort. I perceived he was nervous. After his pitch, I thanked him and walked away politely, reflecting, that he was putting all this pressure on himself. It seemed that he had bound his self-worth and lively-hood to the success of selling this product. Was that true? Did his self-worth correlate to the success of his sales rate?

This man was and is more valuable than anything he sells. He is a kindred spirit, a connected soul, to everyone. Society associates who a person is based on what they do for a living. Is he more valuable than a person who picks up trash for a living or less than a high-ranking business executive? At what point did we make these clear lines of separation between all of us? Do not circumstances define who people are? Of course, but should they?

Value and worth exist for every human. There are many aspects to this. Everyone has a mother, father, a grandfather, and a grandmother. Hopefully, cousins, siblings, aunts, and uncles too. Further, friends are included as family. In this connection that I am making, I hope you see that we are all family.

Being at this conference and noticing all the various roles, I realized my role, and I didn't like it. What came naturally to me, meeting new people and being friendly, all of a sudden seemed difficult. My job was to meet people and network. However, finding myself "trying" seemed impossible. I felt insecure and lost. Who would be the best person to target? What would be the "best" thing to say? The actual human aspect, the best part of me, was lost. I was now in a role, and I wasn't good at it.

The lesson for me was to return to love and to remember who I was—my value and my self-worth. I don't have to play a role, ever. We don't exist to play a role merely. We came to play but as ourselves. The connections I make are genuine; that is the best part. No one is forcing anything, and I am not playing any role. Have you ever tried to put a round peg in a square hole; it doesn't work. Being genuine and in a state of allowance of all things is the way to play in this world. Within this space use your big, loving heart to expand into all areas of your life.

The connections and path that you require will show up for you, at just the right time. All you have to do is love yourself and others. This love will resonate and carry you on your path. It's that easy. Isn't that refreshing? All you have to do is play and bask in the love. Have you ever found that people show up at just the right time without even trying? For example, you may be looking for a realtor and just happen to meet a great one in line at the store. Or you have been looking for your next adventure and your friend invites you on a trip to Peru. These are not coincidences. You attracted this connection at this particular time. Yes, you are that powerful!

When I worked in San Francisco, it was incredible the number of people that I would see every day. Further, everyone looked, dressed, and acted differently. It's quite astonishing how many different people there are. From the outside, they seemed impenetrable, strangers in the vast sea of people. But once I saw a kindred spirit their face would become familiar to me.

I would practice smiling at people on my commute to work. A person that had been a stranger for weeks on a train would become a friend, or, at least, someone that I was comfortable to be around. I love the break in separation between two strangers when a smile is exchanged. It brings a familiarity and comfortableness.

Being open to these types of encounters is pleasing. Of course, only be open to where you feel comfortable. There are times when smiling at people isn't wise. For example, I have learned, sadly, not to smile at certain people because it warrants unwanted behavior. One person wouldn't stop smiling and staring at me for 20 minutes while on public transport. It felt awkward, and that wasn't my intent. It's not to say don't smile; it is to say be wise and listen to your inner knowing when it is a good time to share a smile with a stranger. I made several great friends on that commute just by having a friendly face and being open.

Ironically, problems that humans create are actually an opportunity. The difficulties that are produced need a solution. These issues are a catalyst to connect with others, even nature. For every problem that exists, a solution is required. If the monkeys are losing their rainforest, then this calls for action. This work brings connection. The problem was created by humans. However, the opportunity exists for those who want to fix this issue. The point is that people create and solve their own problems. When this occurs, it brings people together.

All difficulties and solutions are designed to connect and bring people together. That's it. Without problems and solutions, what would you do all day? Sure, it sounds great not to have any problems. I understand. However, isn't it great to have a way to connect with others, at work, at school, and in your home? Considering this requires a shift in thinking. Problems have been given a heavy feeling to them. What if you didn't think of an issue in a negative way but instead as an opportunity to connect with others? How about changing the word "problem" to "opportunity" and see how that looks.

Karen is having a problem with Mike, her husband. It upsets her that she doesn't have more quality time with him. As a result, she is short with him. By behaving this way, Karen only puts more distance between them. Furthermore, this results in even less of a chance that Karen will get the quality time she is seeking. Karen and Mike's problem is that they are having a lack of communication. Let's turn that around. Karen and Mike are having an opportunity. They are both feeling a disconnection, and this is a chance to fix that. One night they end up discussing how they feel. Karen lets Mike know that she is feeling neglected and misses him. Mike says he agrees, and he senses that Karen is always mad at him, not understanding why. Once they communicated the issue they were able to solve it. They both decided to spend 30 minutes most nights focused on each other instead of other things. They were able to communicate and build their relationship by being honest with each other. This whole "problem" was an "opportunity" in their life as it turned things in a better direction for both of them.

When I first married Nate, I understood love at another level. We have been through many ups and downs, and there are more to come. I have been mean, nice, angry, kind, hurt, and healed. Love is ever evolving within each of us. When Nate and I decided to commit to each other on a deeper level, it changed something inside of me. I realized that love is a familial quality. It is this established type of love with Nate that I was opened to more love.

The commitment to love, honor, and respect each other brought a home-like feeling of comfort. I am no longer afraid to love whole-heartedly. I can see things differently. My heart is even more open to the infinite possibility of love.

During our ceremony, The Love Formula was read to remind us of what love is and how it looks. We also had the words by Edmund O'Neill read during our ceremony:

Marriage Joins Two People in the Circle of Its Love

Marriage is a commitment to life, the best that two people can find and bring out in each other. It offers opportunities for sharing and growth that no other relationship can equal. It is a physical and an emotional joining that is promised for a lifetime.

Within the circle of its love, marriage encompasses all of life's most important relationships. A wife and a husband are each other's best friend, confidant, lover, teacher, listener, and critic. And there may come times when one partner is heartbroken or ailing, and the love of the other may resemble the tender caring of a parent for a child.

Marriage deepens and enriches every facet of life. Happiness is fuller, memories are fresher, commitment is stronger, even anger is felt more strongly, and passes away more quickly.

Marriage understands and forgives the mistakes life is unable to avoid. It encourages and nurtures new life, new experiences, and new ways of expressing a love that is deeper than life.

When two people pledge their love and care for each other in marriage, they create a spirit unique unto themselves which binds them closer than any spoken or written words. Marriage is a promise, a potential made in the hearts of two people who love each other and takes a lifetime to fulfill (O'Neill, 2016).

Additionally, here are our vows (from the perspective of me to him):

I, Charissa, take you, Nate, to be my partner, loving what I know of you, and trusting what I do not yet know. I excitedly await the chance to grow together, getting to know the man you will become, and falling in love a little more every day. I promise to love, honor, and be grateful for you through whatever life may bring us. I give you this ring to wear with love and joy. Wear it and think of me and know that I love you.

The foundation of a healthy relationship is love. Knowing what love is and how it looks is the life force of any strong relationship. The joining of two people is a special connection, and with genuine, pure love, it will thrive.

The love of two people goes further than just between husband and wife or girlfriend and boyfriend. Friendship requires love, too. The bond between two friends merits love in action. Lastly, family relationships require actions of love. It is the binding ingredient to healthy and whole relationships. As you learn to love more purely, you open yourself to the beauty of connection with all.

The power of love is reliable, whether for a spouse, mother/father, brother/sister, or a friend. Love feels good and heals. The power of love is infinite. There isn't an official school that teaches how to love. Instead, life is your school. You can use your inner knowing of what feels right and light for you. Further, you can utilize the pure qualities into your love definition.

These qualities are pure because they are infinite as love is infinite. Every iteration of the human race has had the lessons of life that include the pure qualities. All have had lessons about trust, forgiveness, and understanding. All cultures, in all times, have learned about love for others and self-love. This is why I say these qualities are eternal.

Each quality is a piece of the love puzzle as each describes how to love and what love means. Love is gentle and quiet, forgiving, and humble; it gives wise counsel, is patient, trusting, truthful, disciplined, and understanding. The embodiment of love is all of these qualities. Learning these in your life on the small things will spill over into the bigger things. As you practice daily, you will see improvement in all of your relationships including with yourself. Additionally, your spouse will want to be around you more because you will be shining with more love for yourself. This is a beautiful sight to see.

As you practice these qualities of love daily, you will experience more love in your life. How great would it feel to be blanketed in self-love all day long? It puts a smile on your face, right? What if by practicing these qualities, others around you start to make small changes to their love acts? How would this affect you? In this world, you are taught one way to be and act. In the world of love, there is a better way, a deeper, multi-dimensional way. This way is joyful and light. You have the ability to develop with these qualities. You can't change another person, but with the power of love, you can share these powerful tools by being an example.

Love is our purpose in this lifetime. It is love that brings relationships into their full power. The action of love is the catalyst that brings people together. It feels good and light. Love is a very powerful emotion, action, and state of being. When you love others, love is returned to you from the Universe; it may look different than what you expected, but it will return. Love guarantees fruitful relationships and peace.

When you consciously love others, it feels good. This type of giving of love can be a mental hug to a passerby or a kind gesture to a fellow driver on the road. As you continue your love journey, you will be pleased to see how well it works. Next time when sitting in traffic practice love and kindness toward the other drivers and passengers. Potentially, your bad mood will not appear as it usually does. Then, when you arrive home, you may be in a better mood than normal. By practicing love toward others, you are practicing love toward yourself because you can avoid putting yourself in a negative mood. The choice is yours.

Love is an action that needs practice. It may not come quickly for you and that's okay. Continue, or start, kind gestures to co-workers, friends, family, and strangers. Smiling, a mental hug, or a compliment to a store clerk, are all excellent ways of expressing love. What type of love will return to you when you start giving more love?

The Love Formula teaches that there are many aspects to encompass to build a relationship with yourself and others. Here it is again:

The Love Formula

> Love is gentle and quiet; it speaks words of love and kindness and silences "fighting words."

> Love is forgiving; it heals broken hearts and wounds; it is not afraid to say "I'm sorry."

> Love is humble; it believes we are equal and on this journey together.

> Love counsels; it shares wise advice and listens.

> Love is patient; it waits without complaint.

> Love is trusting; it keeps its word and follows through.

Love is truthful; it shares its true feelings, dreams, hopes, and desires. It is authentic.

Love is disciplined; it stays on the path of love, relationship, and health.

Love is understanding; it continually asks questions to know one another through all of life.

As these qualities are infinite so is your life. Your spirit has gone through many evolutions. In each one, you learn about who you are. At some point in your life, you have learned about forgiveness, trust, and love. You have been through many different circumstances and situations, all of which have taught your spirit something. It is in the reflection that you can see the lessons and your growth. Eventually, you will come to know that you are these pure qualities.

I now know that when I look back on my life, I can see all of the lessons of discovering who I am. I am gentle and quiet. I am forgiving. I am humble. I am a counselor. I am patient. I am trusting. I am truthful. I am disciplined. I am understanding. In all of my evolutions, I have learned an important lesson and I get closer to knowing who I am. I am all of these things already; however, I need to discover personally this for myself. Hence, the beautiful thing we call life; our school of discovery of who we are. Truly, we are these pure qualities forever and always.

You are gentle and quiet. You are forgiving. You are humble. You are a counselor. You are patient. You are trusting. You are truthful. You are disciplined. You are understanding.

Cheers to all the love you will experience in your lifetime!

Charissa

The Actionable Love Formula

If you find yourself in any situation, the pure qualities may be used to guide you through to love. They are the basis of love and can be used to lead you on the path that you want for your life. To incorporate the pure qualities in any situation here is a guide:

Gentle and Quiet

Be still and meditate by listening to your inner voice.

Counsel

Seek counsel from those whom you
trust. Follow your knowing and trust the
lightness of what feels right for you.

Patience

Watch the unexpected occur when you are patient.
There is a time for everything. Be patient and
the situation will change. Further, be present and
notice the world around you. When you are patient, the
Universe will deliver what you truly desire.

Self-Discipline

Create positive goals with a plan of action.
Continue doing the activities that are good for
you physically, mentally, and spiritually.

Understanding

Ask questions!

Love

Be kind and gentle with yourself and your situation. Life is a precious adventure to be cherished every moment. The big picture shows that every circumstance is an experience to learn from even if you don't understand why yet. Each chapter in your life completes you. Be filled with love. Be filled with trust.

Lastly, be grateful for all that you have.

References

Chapman, G., & Thomas, J. (2013). When Sorry Isn't Enough. In G. Chapman, & J. Thomas, *When Sorry Isn't Enough* (p. 18). Northfield Press.

Hay, L. (1984). *You Can Heal Your Life.* Carlsbad, CA: Hay House, Inc.

Holy Bible, K. J. (James 1:4). *Bible Gateway.* Retrieved from https://www.biblegateway.com/passage/?search=James+1:4&version=KJV

Holy Bible, N. I. (1 Cor. 13:3). Retrieved from Bible Gateway: https://www.biblegateway.com/passage/?search=1+Corinthians+13:3

Holy Bible, N. I. (1 Cor. 13:4). *Bible Gateway.* Retrieved from https://www.biblegateway.com/passage/?search=1+Corinthians+13

Khayyam, O. (1048-1131). *Good Reads*. Retrieved from Goodreads: https://www.goodreads.com/quotes/22779-be-happy-for-this-moment-this-moment-is-your-life

Menninger, K. (1893-1990). *Brainy Quote*. Retrieved from http://www.brainyquote.com/quotes/quotes/k/karlamenn143978.html

O'Neill, E. (2016, February 18). *Today's Weddings*. Retrieved from http://www.todays-weddings.com/planning/readings/marriage_joins.html

Revenge (2011-2015). [Motion Picture].

Rivers, J. (1933-2014). *Brainy Quotes*. Retrieved from http://www.brainyquote.com/quotes/quotes/j/joanrivers119877.html

Robbins, R. E. (Director). (2013). *Girl Rising* [Motion Picture].

Rosenberg, D. M. (2003). Nonviolent Communication: A Language of Life, 3rd Edition. In D. M. Rosenberg, *Nonviolent Communication: A Language of Life, 3rd Edition*. PuddleDancer Press.

Ward, W. A. (1921-1994). *Good Reads*. Retrieved from Goodreads: https://www.goodreads.com/quotes/353212-forgiveness-is-a-funny-thing-it-warms-the-heart-and

Wilde, O. (1854-1900). *Good Reads*. Retrieved from Goodreads: https://www.goodreads.com/quotes/4583-always-forgive-your-enemies-nothing-annoys-them-so-much

ACKNOWLEDGMENTS

*T*hank you to my father, Ronald Duskis, who was an inspiration for this book. His diligence in seeking and understanding the unique qualities of love led me to dive into studying each quality and applying them to my life.

With all of the love in my heart I'd like to thank my sister and writing coach, Christina Duskis, for her never-ending support, help editing the content, and leading the way by publishing her book, Your Body Relationship (www. ChristinaDuskis.com).

Thank you to my husband, Nate, who has been a path of love and insight. I am grateful for his love, support, and partnership.

My mother, Pina, who is an inspiration and gift. She has devoted many hours of advice and guidance in all aspects of my life. I am deeply grateful for our conversations and special connection.

My mother-in-law, Alanna, who is someone I can count on to guide me into alignment of what I truly desire. Her support is invaluable and deeply appreciated.

And my friends, who bring meaning and purpose to many aspects of my life.

Lastly, thank you to all the open and closed doors that have illuminated my path to where I am today.

About the Author

*C*harissa has read many self-help books about relationships, love, self-acceptance, forgiveness, meditation, and spiritual awareness. Growing up, she was raised as a non-denominational Christian. Her beliefs now stem from a place of spiritual awareness. She is open to learning and receiving insight from the Universe, the Earth, her body, and other people.

The tool she uses the most often is to sense when something feels light or heavy and to follow what feels light. She has learned many tools from the books that she has studied as well as through her experiences. Now she has come up with her own formula to live a life with ease and joy. This recipe is "The Love Formula" to bring about peace and connection with yourself and others in everything that you do—to live a life full of love, adventure, and beautiful relationships.

She believes that love is made up of certain pure qualities. Practicing these qualities will produce stronger, love-filled relationships. Everyone is on a life journey, striving to learn and to be better in their relationships, including the relationship with themselves. This new love formula includes everything that she has learned from many years of researching this topic. She doesn't claim to be perfect or always to practice. However, she does claim to be someone who strives to be loving, kind, and conscientious of her actions and words.

This book is her journey from what she learned and how it can help you with your relationships. Your relationship with yourself and everyone that you are connected to is important. Every relationship that you have aids in your growth of self-love. There are no coincidences, and every person that comes along your path is for a reason. Your journey is unique to you including everyone that you encounter. Navigating your life with love will bring more fulfillment, joy, and ease in all of your relationships including yourself. Her aim is for you to learn about the qualities of love, their benefits, and how to incorporate them into your life to be happy.